Pastor and Parish—
A Systems Approach

E. Mansell Pattison

Fortress Press   Philadelphia

With my deepest love to
Myrna, Stefanie, Stewart, and Benno
who are the system of my existence

Biblical quotations from The Modern Language Bible: The Berkeley Version in Modern English, copyright © 1959, 1969 by Zondervan Publishing House are used by permission.
Biblical quotations from The Living Bible, copyright © 1971 by Tyndale House Publishers, are used by permission.
Materials from the articles "Systems Pastoral Care," by E. Mansell Pattison, originally published in the *Journal of Pastoral Care* 26, no. 1 (March 1972): 2–13; and "Transference and Countertransference in Pastoral Care," originally published in the *Journal of Pastoral Care* 19, no. 4 (Winter 1965): 193–202, are used by permission.

Library of Congress Catalog Card Number 76–62619
ISBN 0–8006–0559–4
Second printing 1981

Contents

65325

Series Foreword

Let me share with you some of the hopes that are in the minds of those of us who helped to develop this series—hopes that relate directly to you as the reader. It is our desire and expectation that these books will be of help to you in developing better working tools as a minister-counselor. We hope that they will do this by encouraging your own creativity in developing more effective methods and programs for helping people live life more fully. It is our intention in this series to affirm the many things you have going for you as a minister in helping troubled persons—the many assets and resources from your religious heritage, your role as the leader of a congregation, and your unique relationship to individuals and families throughout the life cycle. We hope to help you reaffirm the *power of the pastoral* by the use of fresh models and methods in your ministry.

The aim of the series is not to be comprehensive with respect to topics but rather to bring innovative approaches to some major types of counseling. Although the books are practice-oriented, they also provide a solid foundation of theological and psychological insights. They are written primarily for ministers (and those preparing for the ministry) but we hope that they will also prove useful to other counselors who are interested in the crucial role of spiritual and value issues in all helping relationships. In addition we hope that the series will be useful in seminary courses, clergy support groups, continuing education workshops, and lay befriender training.

This is a period of rich new developments in counseling and psychotherapy. The time is ripe for a flowering of creative methods and insights in pastoral care and counseling. Our expectation is that this series will stimulate grass-roots creativity as innovative methods and programs come alive for you. Some of the major thrusts that will be discussed in this series include a new awareness of the unique contributions of the theologically trained counselor, the liberating power of the human potentials orientation, an appreciation of the pastoral-care function of the ministering congregation, the importance of humanizing systems and institutions as well as close relationships, the importance of pastoral *care* (and not just counseling), the many opportunities for caring ministries throughout the life cycle, the deep changes in male-female relationships, and the new psychotherapies such as Gestalt therapy, Transactional Analysis, educative counseling, and crisis methods. Our hope is that this series will enhance your resources for your ministry to persons by opening doorways to understanding of these creative thrusts in pastoral care and counseling.

This volume by E. Mansell Pattison deals with what is potentially the most productive contemporary development in the fields of psychiatry and mental health—the *systems* approach. This approach is useful as a way of understanding and treating human problems. It is also valuable as a way of preventing problems by enhancing the effectiveness of those social systems which nourish human growth. In this book the author applies the systems approach to the life and work of a church, viewing the congregation as a social organism and the minister as a shepherd of this system. In his application of systems theory to parish life Pattison has given us a new set of glasses for seeing pastoral care and nurture as the function of the whole church. (The systemic orientation can help us reaffirm the biblical wisdom which saw the church as a "body" with many interdependent parts.) The author has demonstrated that the systems approach to parish life is indeed a freeing, enabling means of structuring and implementing ministry.

E. Mansell Pattison, M.D., is Professor and Chairman of the Department of Psychiatry, Medical College of Georgia, and Chief of Psychiatry at Talmadge Memorial Hospital, Augusta, Georgia. He has made numerous and significant contributions to our understanding of the mental health role of religious practices and institutions through his extensive research (upon which he draws in this volume) and his prolific writing.

Before his psychiatric career, the author had experience in the ministry. He has sustained an active interest in the church through the years of his work in the mental health field. Pattison is keenly aware of both the complex problems and the rich potentialities of the life of a congregation. He has an appreciation of the struggles of many ministers and of the unique role of pastors in determining the quality of a congregation's systemic climate.

Although the book is directed specifically to parish ministers, its basic concepts can also be used to illuminate other social systems within which ministers function—for example, as chaplains, community change agents, and specialists in pastoral care and counseling. The systems perspective can help one understand and change the *context* of one's ministry. The "shepherd of systems" concept is an invaluable resource in developing a more liberating definition of one's pastoral identity and role, to replace obsolete or limiting definitions. (The book confronts us with the major loss that occurs whenever pastoral counseling becomes the tail that wags the pastoral-care dog.) Pattison's insights will be useful to both pastors and lay leaders of congregations who are committed to developing their churches as more effective environments of growth toward wholeness.

HOWARD J. CLINEBELL

Preface

This book is addressed to the pastor. It is intended as a small contribution to the revitalization of the role of the parish pastor and the reclamation of the church as central to society. I write as one pastor to another.

The background for this book was laid down already in adolescence, in my first experiences as a mission preacher. Since that time I have gone on to a career in academic psychiatry, where I have been fortunate to have repeated opportunities to apply social systems methods in a variety of religious systems. However, my interest is not solely academic, for I have a personal commitment to the message and ministry of the historic Christian church. Some twenty years ago, as I took out my ministerial papers, I hoped to find ways to combine my psychiatric expertise with my dedication to the Christian ministry. The combinations have been kaleidoscopic, and I am thankful for this latest opportunity.

I want to share with fellow ministers a particular way of looking at the church, and at the pastor, which can be called a systems view. I shall deliberately draw upon the scientific framework of social systems theory to address the structure and function of the church. But this is not a scientific analysis alone, for I wish to speak within the framework of the church's historic theology. Accordingly, each chapter begins with a text that will serve as a touchstone to the theological base of the discussion.

I wish to assure you that I harbor no romantic hope either to find or to create an ideal church system. Churches are the creation of people. Like humans, they have life cycles. As living systems, some begin and then abort. Others develop for a time and then remain fixated at a particular point in their developments. Still others mature, grow old, and then die. Churches, like humans, also have differences in temperament, style, and character. As there is no ideal person, so there is no ideal church—each has its strengths and faults. We must all come to respect ourselves for what we are and not demand that we be what we cannot be. We know this to be true of people. It is true also of churches.

There was vitality in the skid-row mission where I first began to preach. There is also vitality in the many forms of the church where I have spoken since: small, huge; city, country; fundamentalist, liberal; pentecostal, liturgical; underground churches, home churches; cathedrals, tents; struggling, affluent; fervent, complacent; denominational, independent; orthodox, heterodox. The total experience has been humbling, for all are living systems. No one church has a corner on vitality.

I am reminded of a street in Hollywood where many types of churches flourish. On one block I saw three church signs. The first sign, the one on the corner, said: The Church of God. The next one, in the middle of the block, said: The True Church of God. The last one, far at the end, said: The Only True Church of God. There was truth in those signs— all of them!

In the profusion of forms we may overlook the essence of the church, its living character. Similarly, the pastor may be identified—perhaps too readily identified—with the particular form of his or her church rather than with the essence of the ministry. I see the pastor as a shepherd—the shepherd of each sheep and the shepherd of the entire flock. Pastoral ministry involves both the nurture of each individual and the care of the whole congregation. In other words, pastoral care is the nurture of the social system of the church. The systems perspective affords a new and helpful way of viewing pastor and parish. Just as the family nurtures each member, so the system of the church should nurture each member. Thus systems pastoral care reaches the individual through the social system of the church. Accordingly, I address this book to the pastor as a shepherd of systems.

1. The Church—A Living System of Identity

I believe . . . in the holy catholic church, the communion of saints.

—The Apostles' Creed

We live today in an individualistic culture. We tend to think atomistically. It seems natural for us to consider life as comprised of discrete units of existence—individual people just like ourselves. It seems unnatural for us to consider organizations or groups of people as fundamental units of existence. As individuals we know ourselves to be alive. We are less confident about collective identity. A group, we feel, does not have a life of its own.

But is that really true? Does not our own speech suggest otherwise? We anthropomorphize groups in statements like: "That group is dead." "The family is learning." "This organization is stupid." Our very language calls into question the individualistic point of view. We may even express our misgivings and say: "Of course a group is not a living thing— it is merely a collection of individual people," but such a rejoinder cannot dismiss the fact that we continue frequently to describe a group in terms of individual human characteristics and behavior.

Actually, our life is like the two sides of a coin. On the one side there is our individual identity, on the other our group identity. Each is reciprocal to the other. Each is a living system and together they constitute a living system. The problem is that in our modern culture we see clearly the individual dimension of our existence but not the group dimension.

1

Identity and the Group

Except perhaps in time of all-out war, when the claims of the nation—and personal loyalties to it—may be all-encompassing, most of us tend to identify ourselves in terms of our individual existence. We see ourselves as persons who join together in groups to form social systems. The individual comes before the group and is constituent of it. Individual identity is viewed as primary, group identity as secondary.

This sense of priority, however, this self-understanding, is peculiar to our time and culture. It is called into question and qualified both by human history as a whole and by the life story of any given individual.

In terms of personal development, it is clear that during childhood our identity begins to take form within the family. The group affords us our first and primary sense of being.

When my son was four years old he went next door one Friday evening to stay overnight with his neighbor friends. We bade him good-night and looked forward to a leisurely opportunity to sleep in on Saturday morning. No such luck! Before 6:30 A.M. the doorbell rang and there stood our bright beaming cherub. "What are you doing here?" I grumped. "Mmm, I'm home" he stated gaily. "I know, but why? Didn't they let you watch TV, feed you, play games, have a good bed?" The little one fidgeted at my stupid questions. In a most matter of fact way he replied: "Oh yeah, we had lots of fun. But I'm home. This is where I am." It was our home—the family—that provided him his sense of being. The experience may be almost universal: first there *is* the family, and only then—and there—*I am*.

Not only child development but history as well underscores how identity is a derivative of the group. Pastors are doubtless familiar with abundant examples.

When the Israelites conquered Jericho, Achan disobeyed God's command and kept some of the spoils. As a result the Israelites fell ill. When Joshua came to Achan's tent and discovered the spoils, judgment was cast not just upon the individual but also upon the primary group: "Joshua took

Achan, and the silver, and the garments, and the wedge of gold, and his sons, and his daughters, and his oxen, and his asses, and his sheep, and his tent, and all that he had. . . . Then all Israel stoned them." (Joshua 7:24–25). Why destroy innocent children and animals? Because of where the sin resided—in the household of Achan. The primary social unit of identity—the sinner—was not so much the individual as the group. Each family member was a reflection *of* as well as a part of this primary unit.

A missionary went to a foreign land to preach the gospel. On the day of arrival he met a tribal chieftain. After a lengthy conversation the chief professed faith in the Christian God. The missionary went to sleep that night thankful for having won his first convert and looking forward to the chance to convert the whole tribe. Early next morning he was awakened by the noise of many people. To his surprise, there before him stood the chief with his 100 tribesmen. "Here," said the chief, "are my Christian tribe." "But wait," said the missionary, "I have not even preached to them yet. They must first hear and then each decide in his own heart for himself." "Oh, no," said the chief. "If I believe, they believe. I am they." The story may be apocryphal, but it does illustrate the difference between our culture's understanding of identity as individual and the understanding in other times and places of identity as group.

In our society at the turn of the twentieth century industrialization brought people from the farms and small towns into the city. People having a group identity in the village suddenly found themselves lost in the anonymous crowds of the metropolitan area. Scholars have sought to describe the resultant phenomenon—masses of individuals having no sense of being. The French sociologist Emile Durkheim spoke of *anomie*—persons who are literally "without name." The American sociologist David Riesman called them "the lonely crowd." Erik Erikson referred to an "identity crisis." Rollo May summed up the dilemma:

> The frontier myth carried the values of not only self-reliance and individual courage, but also objectivity. . . . The gun

that was a tool for self-reliance has now become a tool for
excessive violence. . . . Courageous loneliness has become
neurotic alienation . . rootlessness has become a pressing
problem in that no one has any place to call his own . . .
religion loses its cogency and people are like boats without
any mooring posts. . . . The problem of personal identity
becomes paramount because the means of gaining identity
have evaporated.*

The problem is not simply that we see ourselves as individuals, but that we no longer know *who* we are.   The sources
of our group identity are denied and repressed.   Still, even
though repressed, they return to haunt our lives.   For no life
—no healthy life—is devoid of group identity.

This is seen clearly, for example, in marriage.   Marital
conflict is not merely between two people but also between
two groups.   What happens if a Hatfield marries a McCoy, or
a Montague falls in love with a Capulet?   Romeo and Juliet
are not just two individuals; each has a group identity and a
group loyalty.   Much marital dissatisfaction and tension can
be traced to a conflict between the family identities embedded
in each partner.

When we individualists—people of our time—deny that we
even have a group identity we deny a central dimension of
ourselves.   For human existence is rooted in *two* sources.
Individual identity and group identity are *both* necessary.
They are vital, reciprocal to each other.   Life is not individual
or group but both, and identity must be seen also in its systemic dimensions.

Being and Doing

Human behavior too, in terms of systems theory, must be
regarded as a composite.   It is not exclusively, perhaps not
even primarily, a matter of individual determination.   Indeed,
what we *do* is an expression of what we *are*.   And as identity
must be regarded in terms of components, so behavior must be
understood in terms of the varied influences and factors which
help to shape it.

We may speak of behavior as a *total system* which is itself

* For this and all other notes in this book, see the Notes section
beginning on p. 86.

the product of the several *subsystems* which coalesce in it.*
Each subsystem influences, interacts with, and is reciprocal to
every other subsystem.　Thus no one subsystem determines
what we do; our behavior is rather the resultant of a complex
of forces.　How I spend my Saturday afternoon, for example,
will express the total system of my existence and be determined by the interplay of all the subsystems that influence my
behavior:

> My biological subsystem—whether I am well that day or
> have a cold;
> My psychological subsystem—whether I prefer to read
> professional journals or escape into the joy of gardening;
> My immediate family system—whether we have a family
> picnic planned or each member is occupied with inde-
> pendent pursuits;
> My local community system—whether Saturdays are for
> group work on some neighborhood project or everyone
> goes separately to the beach;
> My geographic system—whether I am in the wintry North
> or the sunny South;
> My economic system—whether my job demands my pres-
> ence even on Saturdays or I work a four-day week;
> My social system of marketing—whether the shopping
> centers are open day and night seven days a week or I
> must finish my shopping before the stores close;
> My religious system—whether I am Jewish, Seventh Day
> Adventist, Mormon, agnostic.

My behavior on any given Saturday will be a function of my
total system at this time.　No subsystem is in itself determina-
tive of the outcome.　For different people, the various subsystems may differ in importance; for the same person their
impact may also vary from time to time.

What happens if there is a change in one subsystem?　Perhaps nothing.　For example, I may have a cold bad enough to
require medication, after which I feel better.　Yet my biologi-
cal subsystem will not determine my Saturday behavior; particularly if my cold has improved I may still participate in the

planned family picnic. On the other hand, if I move from one part of the country to another, I change not only my geographic subsystem but probably also my neighborhood system, my economic system, and my marketing system. Then Saturday becomes a whole new ball game!

What happens when one subsystem is given priority? Behavior and even identity can suffer. If I satisfy my psychological subsystem by reading all afternoon, I may throw my family, neighborhood, and marketing subsystems into disarray. Intrapersonal as well as interpersonal conflict may result. Adjustments will surely be necessary.

Personal behavior is the product of my social system, which is comprised of several subsystems. My social system is not static but dynamic, for a change in any part may require corresponding changes in all the other parts and keep the entire system in flux until it can establish a new equilibrium.

The Living System

Systems theorists have some technical terms for describing these dynamics. They speak of the three principles of a living system: holism, open synergy, and isomorphism.

Holism

The whole is greater than the sum of its parts. The body, for example, is comprised of parts—brain, lungs, liver, heart, limbs—yet we have a living body only when all the parts are organized, connected, and function as a unit. A family is comprised of parts—mother, father, children—yet the parts constitute a family only when the members are joined together and function as an organism. *Holism* has reference to a new and distinct identity, different from that of any of the "parts." A group is not just an assemblage of people gathered together in one room; a group "forms" only when the members actually function out of and in relation to a shared identity. A social system comes into being when the parts are connected together to create a new and unique configuration.

Children enjoy looking into a kaleidoscope, a tubelike viewer toy which has many pieces of colored glass in six sections at one end. As you peer through the tube and rotate it you see the pieces of glass fall into beautiful new patterns. Even so, a social system is a patterned creation made up of parts but greater than the sum of the parts. So we may speak of the "identity" of a social system. Holism points to the distinctness of group identity.

Open Synergy

The parts of the whole work together; they mutually reinforce one another. It is because of this interaction that they together create what could not simply be achieved on a cumulative basis. Bringing parts together into a collection is not the same as bringing them together in organic relationship.

It is said that "two can live as cheaply as one." Two people who create a household can indeed effect economies because the needs of the *pair* are less than the sum of the needs of the two individuals living separately. *Synergy* has reference to the fact that the parts literally "work together." It points to the state which exists when an organization is so arranged that an individual in meeting his or her own needs also meets the needs of other individuals and of the organization.*

In any system the subsystems interact with each other and adjust to one another so that the whole is self-modifying. The system exists in an equilibrium between all the parts, but an equilibrium that is forever changing. The system is not static but grows and moves. This is because the synergy is "open." Change in any one part has impact on every other, and each impact means necessarily further change and new influences in return. The possibilities are kaleidoscopic and the process open-ended.

A family with children is bound to change its form and function over the years, from the time the children are small to the time they are adolescent. A group may change its values, functions, and interactions from the first meeting to the fiftieth. The result of this continuing dynamic, this open-ended interaction, is an emergent purpose that inheres in the system as such rather than in its separate parts. Each social system has its own *directionality*, created by the system as dynamic organism.

Isomorphism

The systemic purpose is shared by all of the subsystems. There is a uniformity about the parts insofar as each partakes of the character and direction of the whole. In a mature group there is a balance between one's individual values and the group values; the group values are shared by each member, even though each member also contributes to the framing of those group values with his or her own individuality. *Isomorphism* has reference to this commonality of shape and purpose among the diverse parts of the whole.

In a family an isomorphic goal may be that of keeping the house clean. Each family member has a specific chore in relation to the overall project, yet each separate task is shaped by and contributes to the common goal of a clean house. Any given action of an individual at cleanup time is likely to resemble in form and character that of the group as a whole.

This principle of isomorphism underscores how each member of the social system has both a unique identity and a shared identity. The actions of the individual members reinforce—and help to shape—the action of the group. Likewise, the action of the system reinforces—and helps to shape —the actions of the individual members.

In summary, the living social system is reciprocal to the life of its members. The members corporately constitute a unique identity—holism. The members interacting create a directional equilibrium—open synergy. The members shape and are shaped by the shared values and goals of the group so that distinct individual actions are consonant (isomorphic) with common group values and goals.

The Church as System

Despite a certain present-day bias against 'the system" or "the institution" in our society, there is value in considering the church under those rubrics. Pastoral care can benefit from the insights of systems theory properly applied.

Primitive food-gathering society was a face-to-face system where everyone interacted with everyone else. Economic, political, family, social, and religious systems were subsystems of the one system in which all participated. As societies evolved, however, specialization of function developed. Within a society organizations emerged as quasi-independent systems. The various organizations had different structures and functions. For our purposes the social systems of which we have been speaking can be classified as organizations,* and a typology developed which will embrace the church as well:

Total institutions organize, circumscribe, and control the entire lives of the members, while providing all basic life-sustaining necessities. Such institutions include prisons, boarding schools, and traditional mental hospitals. Examples within the sphere of the church would be convents and monasteries.

Bureaucratic agencies are governmental. They have regulatory and supervisory functions over the governed, based on legal sanction. Examples are the Census Bureau, Department of Motor Vehicles, and Department of Public Health. Denominational boards might be a counterpart within the field of religion.

Business institutions are organized to deliver a product or service at a profit. The commercial world has them in abundance: cannery, auto plant, consulting firm. Churches may operate a radio station, publishing press, supply stores.

Service agencies are organized to meet a necessary public need, often without profit and on the basis of public subsidy. Every large city has its municipal transit system, garbage collection system, welfare program, and community mental health program. Churches may sponsor a day-care center, youth program, or food and clothing distribution.

Volunteer institutions address themselves to public needs that are not met through the more formal organizations. Frequently they band together for mutual support through a community appeal or united fund. Churches often sponsor some of these volunteer programs and agencies—for shelter, clothing, food, or transportation services.

Self-help groups are less well-organized but serve those forgotten or neglected groups in society which cannot or will not avail themselves of existent service programs. Churches often foster independence and growth by sponsoring or supporting such self-help organizations.

Evanescent organizations represent a response to unmet and poorly identified needs, for a youth drug-counseling center or refugee resettlement. Churches have sometimes been the first to respond to such immediate community needs.

Before the industrial revolution, when most people lived in a face-to-face village lifestyle, the local congregation was a focal point of the community system. The church served a multiplicity of functions: it provided a social structure like unto that of the total institution, significant regulatory and supervisory control of an almost governmental nature, remunerative employment through its ownership of lands engaged in profitable business, a variety of health, welfare, and educational services, and organized voluntary and evanescent services. There was a time in the Western world when the church system was very much *the* community system.

With the rise of the secular state and the attendant development of specialized organizational structures within society, however, the power of the church organization was eroded. Many of its functions were secularized and taken over by other agencies. The loss of these public functions left many people asking, Does the church have any identity? What is its distinctive function?

Two notable reactions were polar opposites: one sounded retreat, holding that the church should and could simply care for its own membership, as in the village theocracy. The church continued to provide social system functions that ran parallel to those of the secular systems. The Mormon Church, hounded to a sanctuary in Utah, is perhaps the best example of this reaction. In a mobile urban culture, however, it is difficult if not impossible to maintain a stable church social system.   So the other reaction was not to buck the trend toward secularization but to join it.   Many of the main-line churches began to sponsor welfare services, health services, volunteer services, and community assistance and help programs.

Both reactions miss the mark if they fail to discern the difference between *being* and *doing*.   From of old, the church as center of the community system combined both being *and* doing.   In modern times, however, as secularization progressed, many of the church's doing dimensions became secularized, and once churchly functions came to be performed by the public and private sector.   The church seemed to have lost its raison d'être.

The Church as the System for Being

Yet the secular institutions that have taken over so many of the doing functions of the church do not necessarily speak to being.   Our culture has so focused attention on doing, that we tend to ignore our being.   And sharing the common preoccupation with doing, church people have all but lost sight of the church as *the* social system for being.

Historically, religious systems offered persons a certainty of life and a security of truth.   The modern age of science, with psychotherapy as its handmaiden, offered a new certainty and a new truth.   Yet the more we advance in the scientific study of humanity the clearer it becomes that we are inverted upon ourselves.   Now science tells us that we *cannot* attain certainty and that we *cannot* know truth.   A psychoanalytic colleague, Allan Wheelis, observes:

> At the beginning of the Modern Age science did, indeed, promise certainty. It does no longer.   Where we now retain the conviction of certainty we do so on our own presumption, while the advancing edge of science warns that absolute truth is a fiction, is a longing of the heart, and not to be had by man. . . .   Our designations of evil are as fallible now as they were ten thousand years ago; we simply are better armed now to act on our fallible visions.*

Although secular social systems have taken over many *doing* functions of the church, they cannot significantly provide *being* functions. This is true of science in general and psychotherapy in particular. Because some secular institutions have attempted to provide a resource for being—and because churches do retain many capacities for doing—it is also true that boundaries are not clear-cut. Nevertheless the church has a special role in relation to human *being*.

Personally and professionally I am concerned about how we create wholeness of life—mental health, if you will. To resurrect an old saying, I would contend that "holiness is wholeness." By this I mean that the church can and should create—be—the social system that produces a whole, holy, person.

This is not to say that members of that system may not be neurotic, psychotic, or subject to the lesser ills of personality distortion; psychologically speaking, all of us *do* better or worse. My concern is rather the quality of *being* that the church can deliver. One can find all sorts of psychopathology among the saints of the church—kings, presidents, managers, workers, and even well-analyzed psychoanalysts. I do not wish to focus on our imperfections, but on the positive quality of who we *are*.

I would not suggest that we neglect the reparative functions of the church, or that psychological dysfunction is of minor concern. But it is precisely the wholesome *system* that will be therapeutic and corrective to its membership. An effective family will heal and care for its members. An effective group will restore its membership to function. Therapy may not be the *goal* of the system, but it can be a *result*. While not denying this, I hold that the primary function of the minister is pastoral care of the social system of the church to the end that the church system can provide the necessary basis for *being*.*

Thus we have seen that identity is based upon both individual *and* group sources of being, and that identity involves both being *and* doing. Although the church shares many *doing* functions with secular systems of society, the church system is a unique source for the *being* dimension of identity.

2. Health and Growth in Living Systems

Encourage one another, therefore, and build up one another, as in fact you are doing. We beg of you, brothers, to recognize the workers among you, those who are leaders in the Lord and your advisers. Because of their work, hold them lovingly in the highest regard. Enjoy peace among yourselves. But we appeal to you, brothers: warn the idle, encourage the fainthearted, give your support to the weak, exercise patience toward everyone. See to it that no one pays back evil for evil; instead, always try to be helpful to one another and to all people.

—1 Thess. 5:11–14 (MLB)

We have seen that individual identity is reciprocal to system identity. It may also be shown that individual health and growth is reciprocal to system health and growth.

Human Development in Group Systems

We are born into a human group—the family. Our first sense of identity is with our parents, then with our brothers and sisters. The toddler's identity enlarges as he comes to feel a part of our house, our yard and eventually our block. The four-year-old may enjoy visiting others, even overnight, but he will rush back home with joy at the earliest opportunity to join his primary group of security and identity.

Then comes the great excursion into the outside world—the kindergarten. As the child moves on into the world of school the individual sense of being is further developed through group interaction in the classroom, on the playground, and with playmates in the neighborhood. The move into adolescence is likewise a group phenomenon, as the parents of any teenager can attest. The adolescent forms his or her ideals, values, clothing preferences, and lifestyle in accord with adolescent group norms.

Moving into adulthood the young person begins to prize his or her individuality, yet continues to look to others for confirmation and support—the sorority or fraternity, the guys who bowl, the girls at the office. Marriage commences with a two-person group which often is subsequently expanded. Young married couples soon band together in neighborhood cliques, kaffeeklatsches, church groups, and sporting and recreational clubs of both formal and informal nature.

In primitive societies, and in our own land when it was primarily rural-agricultural, much of the natural group support, group direction, and group involvement was determined by kinship relationships. We may wistfully recall the large farm families that intermarried and created large clans. In modern times such extended kinship systems have largely vanished. Most middle-class families now consist of mother, father, and young children. These "nuclear" families as they move upward in social class and migrate across the country are relatively cut off from parents and relatives. Yet these families do not exist in social isolation. Though small and set apart, they tend to enter into important relations with other people in their church, their job, their neighborhood. These other people become the *functional* relatives who form the social system of modern life.

Community groups and voluntary associations are often a part of that system. There are service clubs such as Kiwanis or Rotary; fraternal clubs like Moose or Elks; recreational clubs for boating, bowling, or square dancing; social groups centering on a common interest in flowers or books; special-concern groups for parents of retarded children, Gold Star mothers, gay or feminist activists; and self-help groups like Alcoholics Anonymous or Overeaters Anonymous.

Superficially these voluntary community groups may look very dissimilar. In practice they all help people to define the structure of life, evolve solutions to life problems, and deal with life crises.

The Importance of Living Systems

A popular show tune sings of "people who need people." Although the ditty is sentimental, the observation is accurate. The functional effectiveness of our social system is critical to both the physical and emotional well-being of the individual.

The effect of the social system on physical health was first noted in 1904 by Joseph Pratt, the American pioneer of group therapy. While treating tuberculosis patients, he found that their isolation, alienation, shame, and discouragement led to poor response to treatment. So Pratt began to hold classes for the tubercular patients, their families, and their friends. The response was dramatic, for the tubercular patients began to improve as their social systems were activated.*

Sick families tend to generate successive physical illnesses in family members. On the other hand, the social system can be health restoring. In a study of dying patients I found that patients with healthy social systems lived longer, while those with virtually similar physical illnesses but no effective social systems quickly died.†

Similarly, researchers who studied emotional dysfunction over five generations of a family concluded:

> When the individual comes to a therapist for help, we assume that he is admitting the failure of his group as an effective milieu in which to find the solution he seeks to his problems. Our data suggest that the individual seeking help frequently approaches the therapist to protest against the ineffectiveness of the group to which he belongs.‡

Artificial groups contrived for the purposes of psychotherapy are useful but limited. They are limited in that they cannot construct a world of values, ideals, and goals. They are time-limited and space-limited. A therapy group is but one small piece of one's life. In a very real sense therapy groups are for the dropouts who have otherwise failed to establish themselves in effective community groups.

In my own research, I have compared the various natural groups open to most people with several types of psychotherapy groups composed of people needing special help. I found that most natural community groups rate very high on therapeutic elements. They often manifest the important characteristics of a health-growth system: (1) The system embraces the total life of the person. (2) The system has clearly defined values. (3) The system sets specific behaviors for the members. (4) The system models and reinforces desired behaviors. (5) The system allows for learning through catharsis, exploration, and interaction. (6) The system has a high degree of self-generated structure and direction. (7) The leadership is part of the group membership that enables the system to function. (8) The system is semipermeable with community life, so interpenetrating community life—and interpenetrated by it—that the system enhances the members' capacities to function in the community.

Most people in urban society are relatively unaware of the degree to which they rely upon others. Yet our human groups, in a very real sense, can make us or break us. As Cody Marsh, a pioneer in group psychotherapy noted: "By the crowd they have been broken, by the crowd they shall be healed."

The Intimate Psychosocial System

The primary social system for most of us is not just the nuclear family or a community group but a complex network of significant people who form what I call "the intimate psychosocial kinship system." This social system is not an optional superstructure appended to our lives; it is central to effective functioning. Both our physical and mental well-being depend upon the integrity of this system.

Historically, the support system of most people was the entire face-to-face village community. A person was related in one way or another to a system which might comprise as many as a thousand people. This total social system was arranged like a series of concentric circles. The first circle was the immediate family. The second comprised the intimate relatives and friends. These two circles together constituted the extended family kinship system. Beyond that were the third, fourth, and fifth circles of more distant and casual social relations. The first two circles are our immediate concern because for any particular person they comprise the intimate psychosocial system.

The extended family provided two major resources for individual and family sustenance. One resource was *affective* support, that is, emotional involvement, personal interest, and psychological support. The other resource was *instrumental* support, that is, the supply of money, food, clothing, and assistance in daily living and work tasks. The extended family system not only provided these resources but also defined identity, created values, and specified goals. The system provided continuity of identity and values across generations. Thus the extended family, being a part of the church-village social system, was the mediator to individual system members of the overarching religious tenor of life.

During the past century there has been a dramatic change in these primary relationships. The extended-family structure gradually began to be replaced by the nuclear family composed of a mother, father, and those children who have not yet reached their majority. Two factors account for this "nuclearization" of families: technological industrialization and urban migration. Industrialization meant that family vocational traditions, lifestyles and work-styles, could not be maintained over generations. Industrialization led to urban migration, so that people could be "where the jobs were." Thus the young urban families, when they moved, left behind the extended family. They moved geographically, politically, and socially. This loss of the extended-family system deprived the urban nuclear family of both the affective and instrumental resources that had sustained family life. Even more significantly, it deprived the nuclear family of the extended social system that was the source of identity, values, and continuity of existence.

Some theorists, such as sociologist Talcott Parsons, concluded that the nuclear family could not survive as a stable family form because it lacked the stable social system of the extended family.* In part, their dire prediction is reflected in the many contemporary social experiments in marriage and family structure, and the seemingly high vulnerability of the nuclear family as such. Communes and communal living are often an experimental effort to recapture the old extended-family form and benefits.

Rural families, and working-class families in many instances, still manage to retain the extended-family structure. But what has become of the middle-class prototype nuclear family? Middle-class people, even in the cities and suburbs, do not exist in isolation. Sussman has studied how middle-class couples establish coalitions with other middle-class couples to form new quasi-networks that serve the function of the extended-family social system; he reports that "many neolocal nuclear families are closely related within a matrix of mutual assistance and activity which results in a kin-related family system."*

Thus the shift has been away from an extended-family system based on blood or marital relations and toward a new urban-kinship system consisting of family, relatives, friends, neighbors, and associates from work, recreation, and worship.† This new phenomenon is what we refer to as the psychosocial kinship system.

In my own research I have found that individuals select the people who make up their personal system. Selection is based on experienced interaction with the persons and groups involved as well as on the valued importance of each to the individual.

There are five characteristics—five variables—of the interpersonal relationship between a person and those who comprise his or her system:‡ First, the relationship has a relatively high degree of interaction, whether face-to-face, by telephone, or by letter; in other words, a person invests in those with whom one has contact. Second, the relationship is marked by a strong emotional intensity; the degree of investment in others is reflected in the intensity of feeling toward these others. Third, the emotion is positive; negative relationships are maintained only when other factors require it, as in the case of an intolerable boss or an overbearing spouse. Fourth, the relationship has an instrumental base; not only is the other person held in positive emotional regard, but he or she can be counted on for concrete assistance. Fifth, the relationship is symmetrically reciprocal; the other person returns the strong positive feeling and can be counted on for assistance, so that there is both an affective and an instrumental quid pro quo.

I have found that the normal person has about twenty to thirty people in his or her psychosocial system. These relationships are generally rated high on all five variables. There are typically about five or six people in each subgroup of family, relatives, friends, and work-recreation-church associates. About 60 percent of the people in this normal system interact with each other. The person has what might be called a semipermeable network of relationships. Thus the system is not totally closed, although it is relatively stable and consistent.

In contrast, neurotics have only ten to twelve people in their psychosocial systems. Their systems include people who may be dead or live far away. Their ratings on the five variables are much lower than normal, often negative. Only about 30 percent of the system is interconnected. It is as if the neurotic, having a variety of individual relationships, is like the hub of a wheel having spokes that radiate outward but are not connected by a rim. Thus the neurotic has an impoverished psychosocial system.

For psychotics we get a third pattern. Here there are only four to five people in the system. The interpersonal relations are ambivalent and nonreciprocal. The system is 90 to 100 percent interconnected. The psychotic is caught in an exclusive nonpermeable small system that is binding, constrictive, and destructive.

Clearly, then, a psychosocial system does exist for normal urban people today. It is constructed of small subsystems that comprise the larger semipermeable systems. And the characteristic of this psychosocial system, its affective and instrumental supportiveness, is closely related to emotional health. These aspects of our modern life-in-systems are important for servants of the church to know.

3. Functions of the Church System

> You are constructed on the foundation of the apostles and prophets, of which the cornerstone is Christ Jesus. The whole building, framed together in him, rises into a temple that is holy in the Lord, in whom you also are built up together for a dwelling of God in the Spirit.
> —Eph. 2:20–22 (MLB)

The average church exhibits few of the attributes of a well-developed and mature living system. This is because, for most congregations, church structure is at some lesser stage of system development, held together by a pastor who feels overwhelmed by the task of keeping things together and keeping them running. The task is bound to seem overwhelming when one considers the functional losses which have accrued to the church as a result of recent sociocultural change.

Sociocultural Losses

First, as our society has become complex there has been a disruption of the vocational-social-economic-political unity of life. Life has become fragmented. Add to this the geographic dispersion of a congregation's membership, and we see a disruption of the opportunity for cohesive interaction throughout different spheres of daily living. Not infrequently even the youth of the church attend different grade and high schools.

Second, this disruption of cohesive interaction diminishes the opportunity to develop strong emotional bonds between people. Feelings are generated by interaction. Emotional bonds are built on meaningful interchange and collaboration. Absence does not make the heart grow fonder. The strongest emotional bondings occur between people who have multiple spheres of interaction, who repeatedly and in different contexts have to do directly with each other. Casual, intermittent meetings of people who have nothing to share except a worship service do not build emotional bonds.

Third, the interpersonal bonds, to no small degree, are diminished as a result of the loss of instrumental tasks to perform. The church has suffered attrition in its instrumental functions as they have been taken over by secular agencies. Thereby the members of the church have lost an important factor in the development of interpersonal relations. The strongest interpersonal bonds occur when there is a combination of both affective *and* instrumental elements in the relationship. People who play, pray, and work together stay together.

Fourth, there has been a loss of symmetrical reciprocity. That is, the withdrawal into personal isolation and nuclear-family isolation prevents people from expressing their feelings and life needs. Moreover, people have no system of communication whereby they can become aware of the needs of others. Hospitalizations, even funerals can occur in some congregations without the members ever knowing of it. To this we must add the contemporary ethos of self-sufficiency: we tend to assume that we need no one and that we should take care of ourselves—and that others should do likewise! Although we may give to others in need, particularly if they are known to us directly, there is a vein of latent hostility toward those in our midst who are not self-sufficient. Yet effective interpersonal relations are built upon the ongoing *exchange* of emotional and instrumental assistance. From a systems view, one may say, "It is more blessed to give *and* to receive."

Systemic Weaknesses

Some of the problems of the overwhelmed pastor inhere in the very nature of congregational life as it is manifest among us today. Many churches, perhaps most churches, resemble more an artificial than a natural system. They may refer to themselves as "families" but in fact they have greater affinity with the therapy groups to which I earlier referred.

Natural systems can have more intrinsic health and growth potential than any artificial therapeutic system. This is because effective natural systems are characterized by:

  —multiple interactions
    —in many spheres of life activity
      —over continuing and varied times and places
        —that involve affective and instrumental dimensions
          —between people with multiple connections to each other.

It helps to see each of these aspects in terms of its unique importance for the strength and effectiveness of the system.

By contrast the average church system in which pastors find themselves laboring today is characterized by:

  —single interactions
    —in one sphere of life
      —usually at one time and in one place
        —that involve little affective or instrumental exchange
          —between people with few connections.

It is obvious that such a system will, as a living system, be comparatively weak and ineffectual. Where people hardly know each other's names a pastor is bound to be overloaded with more tasks and responsibilities than one person can ever hope to perform.

Any affirmative action in the face of such a situation must be informed by a view of the desired end. Recalling the losses that have occurred as a result of sociocultural change, and the strengths that typically characterize the natural social system, it is possible to enumerate eight dimensions or functions of the strong living system as they pertain specifically to the church.

Functions of a Strong Church System

Leadership

The church system must provide leadership. There can be no system without leadership. That leadership begins, but does not end, with the pastor.

The leadership functions to provide three main things: ideas, means of action, and coordination. Usually, the idea person, the implementation person, and the coordination person are not embodied in the same individual.

Good leadership involves enabling many people to assume leadership, and vesting in them the requisite authority and responsibility. It means sharing of leadership roles and functions. The best leader acts as leader in one area and follower in another. The system must build leadership.

Commitment

The church system must provide commitment. There is a vacuum in our society. We lack a system that defines our common identity, values, goals, faith, and hope.

The siren of secular acceptability has decimated the commitment of the church. It has seduced religion into adopting the goals and values of scientific, psychological, and sociological sophisticates. The devout person, the person who stands for something, has almost become a social anachronism. Yet it is noteworthy that young people today are no longer interested in the dead and empty humanism of religiosity. They look for a place, a belief, a value, to which they can commit themselves. Young people see clearly that we have sold out faithful commitment, and they are yelling loudly that "the church (like the fabled Emperor) has no clothes."

Thus the church system must clearly stand for a view of creation, of life, and of identity. This commitment is the shared identity that forms the cohesive ground of the system.

Behavioral Sanctions

The church system must sanction specific attitudes and behaviors. Personal relations are built on principles. I say to my spouse, "I love you—I am committed to you." That commitment stands behind and gives fundamental, enduring support to the vagaries, the ups-and-downs of daily interaction between us.

But the actualization and realization of that principle comes in specific actions. I request specific things of you, and you request specific things of me. Human relationships are not a matter of laissez-faire.

When I speak up for specificity, I do not mean to imply arbitrariness, nor do I exclude the necessity for negotiation, compromise, and mutual acceptance. I wish only to indicate that a strong interpersonal relationship involves the right to ask for and to receive, to demand and to acquiesce.

Ineffective, weak systems present nonspecific generalities that do not define precise expectations for its members. The church system must engage in precise dialogue with respect to the expectations of its membership.

Organization

The church system must provide organization. Effective systems have well-established organization.

Organization provides ease of access for new members without placing undue immediate demands upon them. It provides for lateral and vertical mobility to accomplish tasks; for learning and growth into positions of leadership; for the sharing of leadership, responsibility, and authority; for an orderly division of labor. And it provides the means whereby the system can generate direction and achieve specific goals.

Goals and Tasks

The church system must provide specific goals and tasks. These afford opportunity for people to do things together. In doing shared tasks, people build interpersonal relationships. The most effective systems have specified goals, and well-organized tasks devoted to achieving those goals.

Freud defined "mental health" as *arbeiten und lieben*—the capacity to love and to work. Work is an arena for identity development and identity reinforcement; shared work supports both system identity and individual identity.

System work is vital to an effective system. A passive system that requires nothing of its members is a weak and ineffective system. An active generative system feeds on its own accomplishments.

Association

The church system must provide for association. The opposite of work is play. In our achievement-oriented culture we tend to denigrate leisure time and casual conversation, but play is essential for existence.

In play we do several things. We rest and recuperate; surely we need that. But there is more: in play we allow for reintegration of ourselves. When attention is centered on goals and work our focus is necessarily constricted; we lose perspective on ourselves. In play, however, we not only have opportunity to regain perspective; we also get in touch with the wholeness of ourselves.

By play I mean not only recreation, games, and entertainment, I mean also other activity that is not goal-directed but engaged in for the pleasure it affords in its own right, and for the opportunity for casual association between people. Historically this has meant, for the church, such things as kaffeeklatsches, receptions, dinners, picnics, and the casual socialization which attends such events. Human relationships are built on more than working together.

Occasions for association allow us emotionally to feed on one another. The old-fashioned wake was a good example of this; the mourners came to the house of the bereaved to share speech, silence, and refreshments.

But it is not just in times of crisis that we need association. The most effective systems engage in a good deal of nonstructured casual togetherness. Some of the most important and meaningful personal interactions take place in these casual associations.

One of the characteristics of an effective natural system is that it does not have special times for important emotional exchanges between people. Rather there is frequent opportunity for brief emotional exchanges in many settings and circumstances. An interesting example is the pattern of communication within the family. Some of the most important parent-child interactions occur in the casual atmosphere of the dinner table. The very casualness allows serious issues to be raised and resolved without arousing anxiety and tension. In this casualness there is the freedom for interchange.

Thus the church system must provide for association and togetherness. There must be multiple opportunities not just for work but also for play, entertainment, and casual association among the members.

Behavioral Taboos

The church system must provide taboos in the areas of sex and aggression. The traditional extended kinship system established and reinforced limits on the behavior of its members. There is no freedom without limits. The setting of limits, or the establishment of taboos, gives clarity to behavior, for only then does one know what is acceptable and what is not. In short, people need to know how to respond to each other.

Today we have no clear procedures for establishing relationships with people beyond the pale of blood or marital connections. This is in contrast to most nontechnological cultures which have many mechanisms for labeling people as honorary aunts, great-uncles, kissing cousins, and best friends. We have no way to define neighbors, friends, and associates as kin—a definition which would create the necessary taboos. Thus there is no way to know if you are being too aggressive or not aggressive enough. There is no way to know what to ask of others and what to expect in return. There is no way to develop emotional intimacy without risking misinterpreted sexualization.

For the church system to function effectively it must establish "named relationships" between its members, relationships that carry with them definitions of both rights and expectations, but also aggressive and sexual taboos. We see modest examples of this in the life of the church: the tradition of naming "godparents" establishes one kind of relationship; and the churches in which members call each other "brother" or "sister" circumscribe such relationships with taboos both positive and negative. But these are comparatively weak attempts in the right direction. There is a challenge in this area for the churches to create the *possibilities for intimacy.*

Outside Connections

The church system must provide semipermeable relationships with the outside community. The church is not the same as the community or neighborhood or area in which it exists. Nor can the church be a self-contained community, complete and sufficient unto itself. There must be a flow of interaction and influence—there must be connections—between the church system and the community system. Effective systems enable their members to relate more effectively to the larger community experiences—the other systems—in which its members are caught up.

The family is a good example of this principle. An effective family prepares its members to go out into the community during the day, and then receives the family back together in the evening. The family becomes the system for preparation and for replenishment. The family that is a closed system is functionally less effective. The psychotic system, as we have seen, is a closed, impermeable system.

So the church system must be linked through many connections to the ongoing life of the surrounding and encroaching community. A church system that is out of touch with its community will inevitably fail to prepare its membership for life in the outside community.

These are eight dimensions and functions of an effective social system. The church as living system functions best when it provides leadership, commitment, behavioral sanctions, organization, goals and tasks, association, behavioral taboos, and outside connections. These are crucial functions of the healthy—and health-engendering—system, and must be regarded as optimum contributions of the effective church.

4. The Subsystems of the Church

Our bodies have many parts, but the many parts make up only one body when they are all put together. So it is with the "body" of Christ. . . .
And some of the parts that seem weakest and least important are really the most necessary. Yes, we are especially glad to have some parts that seem rather odd! . . . This makes for happiness among the parts, so that the parts have the same care for each other that they do for themselves. If one part suffers, all parts suffer with it, and if one part is honored, all the parts are glad. . . . All of you together are the one body of Christ and each one of you is a separate and necessary part of it.

—1 Cor. 12:12–27 (LB)

We have been examining thus far the system as a whole. It is time now to look at the parts of the system.

In a living system each part, or subsystem, has its special function. No one subsystem has priority over the other. Each reciprocally supports the other. Individually and collectively the subsystems contribute to the whole.

The church as a living system contributes to the lives of its members. The system as a whole does this best when each subsystem is functioning at its best and contributing to the functioning of the whole. It is important for the minister to be aware of the nature and functioning of each subsystem.

The Proclaiming Subsystem

Every age and every society has its world view, its a priori definitions of the universe and the place of humanity in it. Traditionally the church has always been a major source of such a world view. But the church's proclamation has lately been lost in pluralism and the dilemma of changing world views.

Changing World Views

At the turn of the twentieth century the majority of the population lived in small towns and villages. Even for those who lived in urban areas the ethnic neighborhood functioned effectively as a small town. The local community, relatively small and relatively homogeneous, was a "mono-valued" culture in which everyone lived the same way, felt the same way, thought the same way, existed the same way. Although these small cultures changed, they changed slowly, naturally, almost imperceptibly, as if things were meant to be as they were.

A person born into such a small, restricted culture grew up with an experience of the world about that was consistent and uniform—and clear. Unconsciously, from infancy on, the values, mores, and patterns of *beingness* were taken in and absorbed, cemented into the child's ego structuring of the world. Like an arrow shot from a sure bow, children grew up the way they should. The trajectory of their becoming was fixed. They became "good" persons.

As a result, the person growing up in this "world" acquired an ego structure of reality that was firm and sure. There was an intrinsic sense of goodness and truth. One *knew* what was right and wrong, acceptable and vile, desirable and loathsome. When decisions were to be made one did not appeal to logic, to evidence, to experimentation first of all. One simply looked inside oneself, to one's own feelings, one's own internal sense of "knownness"—to that which cannot be gainsaid by innovative external ideas. One *knew* what the right decision should be. For how can anything controvert the reality that is a part of oneself? This was the social system about the turn of the century, not much different from what it had been for centuries, even millenia before. Being, behavior, and relationship were all of a piece, laid down by the world view of the mono-valued culture. But changes were brewing about the turn of the century, in no small measure occasioned by radical new developments in technology. Young men and women began leaving the small town. They also left their urban ghettos and boroughs. An increasingly mobile population came to discover that the world view of their upbringing was chauvinistic, provincial, naive, indeed religious! And so they learned a *new* world view. They appropriated a world view based on rationalism, empiricism, scientism. Forsaking the faith of their elders, they followed the faith of the new prophets. Thus we arrive at the dominant world view of the twentieth century. The scientific professional person today, no longer beholden to the myths, fantasies, and superstitions of religious forbears, is presumably free! "Modern" people had traded the mono-valued culture of the small town for the mono-valued culture of cosmopolitan science.

Pluralism

Yet even science cannot supply the lost security and continuity of yesteryear's local community. The majority of people now live in a handful of large megalopoli. People who came from different mono-valued cultures find themselves living, working, existing side-by-side with people who are different from themselves—people whom they do not understand, people with whom they do not agree, people who do not live as they do. And so it happens that today, more likely than not, my next-door neighbor, instead of sharing my world view, calls it into question. Far from providing stability and support, the people in my block actually challenge the very essence of my existence.

In our quest for answers to the meaning of life, and for guidance on how to live it, we look almost in vain to the people about us for reinforcement and reassurance. We need the security of feeling that our way of living life is right, true, valuable, and meaningful. We need to know that we have something worth bequeathing to our children. Yes, it is a bewildering affair today, trying to decide how to raise our children. We can demand that they follow precisely in our footsteps, but that is gauche. So we say to them instead: "Make up your own mind, we cannot guide you." As a result, children grow up without any parental commitment to a lifestyle of their own and having carte blanche to choose their own lifestyle. As a result, our children feel lost and confused.

They look to us for a way to *be*. They reach out, grasping for a path to being-in-the-world that will give them direction, certainty, satisfaction, and meaning. And what they find is bewildering variety and directionless "freedom" to choose.

Heretofore, in the history of the human race, ego development and the ego sense of reality have been based upon a normative view of the world. Now we are faced with the pluralism of human existence. There are *many* ways to be-in-the-world. Yet each of us can only espouse one way. The world views may be plural, but *I* am one. *I* must choose *one* way to be. And that way, though it may not be normative for others, must be normative for me.

The Dilemma

So how do we decide to live out our lives? How do we pick our way through the jungled maze of existence? How do we make a path through the forest?

In the earliest times, in primary societies, and in the major human cultures the way to live life was spelled out in terms of religion. Religion was the overarching superstructure that embodied how one should live. From the earliest times to the present, religious frames of reference have served to structure human existence.*

With the advent of the scientific age, however, religion was seen as superfluous, constricting, and destructive. Science would replace religion. To twentieth-century professional people, the idea of religion was atavistic, primitive. And if we must have religion, we should at least make it scientifically respectable.

But the scientific way, as we have seen, turned out to be no way at all. Whereas the religious systems of human guidance offered people a certainty of life and a security of truth that, from a scientific perspective, was held to be archaic, science promised the benefits of a new certainty and a new truth. But what science promised it could not deliver.

So where does that leave us? We can no longer pretend. We see clearly in our consciousness that we stand naked in the world. Nietzsche is said to have run in the streets crying,

"Fall on your knees and weep, for God is dead!" And, following him, the preeminent philosopher of our times, Jean
Paul Sartre, looked out on the streets of science and saw that
science too was dead! So after all, one is alone, desolate,
forlorn. One has nowhere to turn to find out how to *be*.

Proclamation

It is to this existential dilemma of being that the church
must speak today. It must offer a proclamation that can give
foundation, substance, and integrity to being, behavior, and
relationship.

It is unfashionable these days to be dogmatic. Yet the
church that speaks to everyone speaks to no one. In its proclaiming function the church must answer to the need for a
central "ground of being" for both individual and corporate
existence. The individual affirmation of self is a lonely if not
impossible task. Thus basic to the proclamation of the church
must be a corporate identity and a corporate proclamation.
We proclaim who we *are*, and we do so within a historic
church tradition that provides both the *context* and the *con-
tent* for assured and meaningful proclamation.

The proclamation of the church must speak to three basic
dimensions of existence: historical continuity, behavioral
actualization, and person-building relationship. All three
dimensions are symbolized as well as affirmed in the traditional liturgy of the church.

First, the reading of the Old Testament proclaims the enduring commitment of God to his people. It affirms the historic continuity of the people of God with each other and with
their Creator. Whatever its locus in the scheme of time and
history, at any given moment the congregation is grounded
and has its being in the historic church which was before and
shall continue. Its identity is grounded in historical continuity. Thus grounded, the church, through its proclamation,
imparts to persons a transcendent sense of belonging, an identity that is not ephemeral but has staying power.

Second, the reading of the Epistle spells out explicit biblical patterns of everyday life and interpersonal behavior. Here is affirmation of standards past and commitment to future actualization. Here being is translated into behavior. And while doing may depend upon being, what we *are* is in no small measure influenced by what we *do*. In its proclamation, the church guiding people in their *doing* can help them to *be*. It can help to actualize being.

Third, the reading of the Gospel makes the whole thing personal. Here the transcendent God is made immanent in us. Here is the existential immediacy of my being a child of God. And the proclaimed Relation which connects me with Ultimate Reality *enables* all the other relationships which integrate, embed, and incorporate me in life itself. The child in the family finds similar grounding, support, and affirmation in the home, where identity is shaped. In a context of love communicated the child is given an identity that involves historical continuity with self and forbears, behavioral actualization in terms of commitments and standards, and experienced relationships which engender meaningful personhood. The church functions in like manner, even at the core of its established worship patterns, to address all three dimensions of identity. This is the function of its proclaiming subsystem.

The Symbolizing Subsystem

It was Alfred North Whitehead who noted that the vitality of a culture is reflected in its symbols, for as society changes it must reconstitute its sense of being. This means that in every generation a society must resymbolize its existence. This is true also for every living system, including the church.

Signs and Symbols

There is a difference between symbols and signs. A sign is commonplace, having an almost universal and widely agreed-upon meaning. It represents something. A sign is a direct representative of what it refers to. Different semaphore flag positions, for example, stand for different letters of the alphabet. Morse code is comprised of signs. A barber pole is a sign. Its very presence serves as an indicator, and when it is rotating it signifies something even more important to the person needing a haircut.

A symbol, on the contrary, is not merely an indicator; it is a purveyor of power. It does not just represent; it is pregnant with meaning. A symbol takes a universe of experience, synthesizes and integrates that universe into a succinct form, and evokes a powerful response. A white flag of truce is a symbol. It brings together the situations of the combatants, integrates them into a single event, and evokes urgent responses from both sides.

Social systems rely more on symbols than on signs, as any effective leader will attest. Hitler and his crowds shout "Heil," Churchill waved his fingers in a "V" for victory, while Martin Luther King led his marchers in singing "We shall overcome." Control of the symbols leads to control of the system. This is why groups will even fight for symbols.

As patriotism began to wane in the United States following the Second World War, people no longer doffed their hats as the Stars and Stripes passed by on parade with the band tooting Cohan's "It's a Grand Old Flag." But when the Vietnam War provoked the latent conflict over social change in America, the flag was reinvested with symbolic power. Avant-garde young people painted the flag on their VW buses, spread the flag as their tablecloth, and sewed clothes from flags. What they intended was not desecration but revitalization. Their concern was to reform the country, and they symbolized that concern by making the symbol an intimate part of their lives. At the same time, conservative people expressed their concern for the country by flying the flag, wearing it on their lapel pins, sewing flags on their uniforms, and putting flag stickers on their cars. Thus both groups grasped for the same symbol. But was the banner to symbolize change and reform or conservation and steadfastness? Here we see the same flag being used to symbolize the same overall situation but evoking two different calls for response in two different groups.

Unlike a sign—think of the latest international road and

highway markers being installed to instruct and direct motorists—a symbol does not contain universal meaning. Rather a group *invests* a symbol with meaning. And that meaning is powerful, not merely informative; it makes a difference!

At a birthday party there are presents and games, cake and candles. We sing "Happy Birthday," the candles are blown out, the cake is eaten, and the gifts opened. This is what is *done*. This is the action. But what do the acts *mean*? What has *happened*? To reduce the totality of the event to words, we might put it like this: "We recognize your growth, dear child. We affirm our commitment and relationship to you. In this moment we gather together all the feelings we have toward you, and yours toward us. We pledge our ongoing life together as a family that supports and sustains you." The simple actions say all of that. A mundane event, the party calls forth the basic commitment, reaffirms the relationship, and evokes a sustaining response that involves both being and behavior. The candles may be a sign indicating age, but the birthday party as such is a powerful symbol.

The Power of the Symbol

Rollo May expresses well the function of symbolizing:

> The symbol draws together and unites an experience. It bridges the inescapable antimonies of life—conscious and unconscious, reason and emotion, individual and society, history and the present. For example, the Christian cross draws together the horizontal and vertical dimensions of life and unites them perpendicularly to each other, embracing their conflict. A symbol is real and efficacious only to those who commit themselves to it.*

A living system is a symbolizing system. Therefore the church must be actively engaged in creating symbols and investing them with meaning and power. This is an ongoing process. The symbols of the church are varied. They may be a liturgical chant or a doxology, shaking hands in the pew in the middle of the service or speaking in tongues, testimonies or silent prayers, the vestments that are worn or the absence of

special vestments. Some of the symbols are the heritage of a
rich tradition; some are the creation of a creative minister.

What is symbolic in one congregation may be meaningless
in another. Each congregation or group of congregations
must symbolize its own existence, and resymbolize it as
changes occur over periods of time. But symbolize the
church *will*, and symbolize it *must*, for in this way the church
forms, nurtures, sums up, and articulates life and the meaning
of life for its people.

The Moralizing Subsystem

The Second World War convulsed the world both physi-
cally and morally. In the aftermath of its antecedent and
attendant atrocities came a determined attempt to assess the
moral dilemma of the world and assert a world moral order.
The focus of this reassessment occurred in the Nuremburg war-
crimes trials, in which two opposing moral positions were
brought face to face. The defendants argued that they were
merely implementing directives and thereby actually obeying
the laws of the land; the prosecution argued in reply that certain basic human rights and responsibilities are—and always
were—self-evident and inviolable, not to be breached even out
of "obedience to laws of the land." The issue was clear: Are
there universal norms—absolutes—of human morality, or
does each society construct its own—relative—system of
morality?

The Societal Aspect of Morality

Much of our thinking about morality has been formulated
in personal terms. We are fond of quoting Martin Luther, the
lonely monk standing at the bar of the Empire: "Here I stand,
I can do no other." Often his stance has been interpreted as
pitting the individual conscience against the established pow-
ers or forces of society. Yet this interpretation misconstrues
the essential nature of morality, which is simultaneously both
a personal and a social concern.

Clyde Kluckhohn, the late Harvard anthropologist, summed
up the matter well:

There is the need for a moral order. Human life is necessarily a moral life precisely because it is a social life, and in the case of the human animal the minimum requirements for predictability of social behavior that will insure some stability and continuity are not taken care of automatically by biologically inherited instincts, as with the bees and the ants. Hence, there must be generally accepted standards of conduct, and these values are more compelling if they are invested with divine authority and continually symbolized in rites that appeal to the senses.*

No society, then, can function without a specific morality. The system, of course, is shaped by moral individuals. But the system also shapes morals. Morality is not a question merely of specific prohibitions or imperatives; it is rather that composite of values and definitions of what is appropriate by which we as individuals govern our behavior in society—and protest against social mores and injustice.

Morality as Process

For too long we have seen the morality of a society in static terms, as something fixed and unchanging. But morality must be a process, for society is always in a process of flux, revision and development. New moral decisions for human relations and actions must be negotiated and renegotiated.

The understanding of morality as process underscores the importance—indeed the necessity—of "new morality," not just today but in every age. Jesus understood the Ten Commandments by which he was raised as negative definitions of love; they spell out some, though not all, the conditions of nonlove. He enunciated a "new commandment" when he focused on the positive affirmations and demands of *love.*

We can affirm an ethic of absoluteness. But this affirmation of absolute moral norms does not help us solve life's problems. Our absolute moral norms are broad general principles, but life requires greater specificity and concreteness in decision and action. Specific interpersonal pieces of behavior are not self-evident, but vary with time, place, and culture.

Stealing, for example, is generally regarded as a violation of human relationships. Yet in certain South Sea Islands people leave their coats outside their huts for the use of any passerby who needs a coat—whereas in our society one would be upset if a stranger took one's coat from the cloakroom at the opera, or the church! To shoot a horse thief was appropriate moral behavior in the Old West, but not in the New West with its alternative means of transportation. In other words, for all our commitment to the highest universal ethical standards, we are faced with the perpetual task of defining what the dictates of love, or the Decalogue, require in the conditions of our time, our place, our society. We have to apply our absolute moral norms in a manner relative to the society at hand.

Relative Absolutes

That relative definition, however, must be treated as an absolute standard. Decisions of the Supreme Court, for example, while rooted in an absolute, the Constitution, clearly grow out of and are applicable to specified situations—for which they are then ultimately binding. To the Court are brought all sorts of moral issues which come under the jurisdiction of the law. The Court makes a ruling as to the most appropriate moral resolution in the light of available evidence. The people then act—if need be are compelled to act—according to that ruling until the same dilemma is brought to the Court for renewed evaluation and a revised moral/legal ruling. It is recognized that the Supreme Court is not handing down a "final" decision, but rather the best decision that can be made at this time.

In terms of school segregation for example, the "separate but equal" doctrine of the late nineteenth century was the best moral decision that could be achieved in that time and context, but a new moral doctrine necessarily prevails in the twentieth century. We can even expect that the whole issue will be reevaluated in the decades ahead.

It is important to note that the Supreme Court still follows a set of moral absolutes—the Constitution. The moral problem is not one of absolutes, but how to apply the absolutes within the relativities of a framework of society, and then enforce the relative standards absolutely.

Morality and Development

The relationship between individual and social morality can also be looked at in terms of personal development. The small child first learns morality as a personal, idiosyncratic set of behaviors; only later does there begin to develop a more generalizable and universal set of values. Lawrence Kohlberg has constructed a scale of moral development that consists of six stages or orientations that coordinate with developing levels of personal maturity: *

> Stage 1: Obedience and punishment orientation. Egocentric deference to superior power or prestige. Emphasis on avoiding trouble.
>
> Stage 2: Naively egoistic orientation. Right action as an instrument of self-satisfaction. Emphasis on satisfying one's own needs, and occasionally the needs of others.
>
> Stage 3: Good-person orientation. The quest for approval. Emphasis on pleasing and helping others.
>
> Stage 4: Authority and social-order orientation. "Doing one's duty." Emphasis on showing respect for authority and on maintaining the given social order for its own sake.
>
> Stage 5: Contractual-legalistic orientation. Duty defined in terms of others. Emphasis on majority will and societal welfare.
>
> Stage 6: Conscious principle orientation. Appeal to logical universality and consistency. Emphasis not only on actually ordained social rules but on principles of choice.

Kohlberg has found that most individuals usually operate at the more immature stages of morality. The result is extensive, even debilitating confusion on the part of people whose general social institutions—the secular courts and the more reflective ethical theology—focus on and operate on the basis of Stage 6 morality. Even common Christian morality has frequently been framed in terms of the lowest levels of morality (avoidance for fear of punishment, egoistic self-seeking rather than in terms of the highest levels of morality (societal well-being, commitment to responsible application of principle).

The Church as Moral Innovator

Milton Rokeach, one of the foremost research psychologists in the area of values, comments on this problem:

> If religious institutions taken as a whole are indeed, at best, irrelevant and, at worst, training centers for hypocrisy, indifference, and callousness, it is unlikely that those who are part of the Religious Establishment will voluntarily initiate the program of radical change that seems called for. . . . If a way can be found to reverse the emphasis between proscriptive and prescriptive learning, children can be taught that salvation is a reward for obeying the "thou shalts" of the Sermon on the Mount, rather than the "thou shalt nots" of the Ten Commandments. Such a simple shift of focus, however, would probably require a profound reorganization of the total social structure of organized Christian religions. And if such a reorganization turns out to be too difficult to bring about because of rigidity, dogmatism, or vested interest, the data presented here lead me to propose that man's relations to his fellowman will probably thrive at least a bit more if he altogether forgets or unlearns or ignores what organized religion has tried to teach about values and what values are for.*

Such pessimism is unwarranted, but the warning must be heeded. The Christian church is always of a particular time and place; yet it is readily encrusted with a sense of permanence and "rightness." Thus there is the ever-present danger that the church and its morality can become simply a defender of the status quo. One of the traditional roles of the church has been that of definer, sustainer, and enforcer of moral values, values which have a proven heritage of worth and a more than ephemeral ground. That in itself is good. But the fact that many churches have come to be regarded exclusively as bastions for the defense of the status quo is cause for dismay.

What has been overlooked is the need for challenge and change in morals, not merely the maintenance of morals. The church has become primarily an agent for the maintenance of outmoded moralities and has lost its function as a shaper of new moralities. Thus, it has lost half of its relevance as a moral agent. There must be a renaissance, a fresh attempt to reclaim the role of the church as moral innovator in society.

Christian Freedom

The Christian religion promises "freedom in Christ" but instead it has often produced church members hounded by fear, guilt, and anxiety. The message of Christ affirms the reconciliation of man to his Creator, thus affirming man's opportunity freely to choose his life without condemnation. The "man in Christ" no longer has to justify his existence. Yet we shrink from that freedom to be and to choose.

I returned from a trip one time with a bag of lollipops for my children. They pranced impatiently as I opened the sack and held out the goodies. But then, suddenly, they hesitated: "Daddy, which one shall I choose? Will I like the green one or the purple one? Daddy, you know best, tell me which one to take—I don't want to take one I won't like!" But I refused to tell. The choice was theirs. They must select their own lollipops and then live with the consequences. Faced with such fateful choice the children backed off. Tears welled up in their eyes. In anger they pouted and refused the lollipops altogether. They did not want their freedom! They did not want to take the responsibility—and the consequences—for making a choice that could be wrong.

Too often the church system has taken the position of telling its members how and what to choose, as if the system had the answer to the best lollipop. And the members, like children of an overprotective parent, have bought this security of the system. I am reminded of Eric Fromm's comment in *Escape From Freedom* that people would rather have the security of false truth than the freedom of ambiguous reality.*

Thus I see the church as a center for moral dialogue, affording people opportunity for examination and reexamination of the ever-new moral dilemmas of life. The moralizing subsystem of the church is both a maintainer of an ongoing commitment to universal moral norms, and a moral innovator bringing forth new responses to changing dilemmas.

The Learning-Growth Subsystem

In our culture we tend to see learning and growth as painful and onerous, something to be required of children but not of grownups. When we become adults we no longer have to learn or grow; we are excused. But is not the reverse the truth? If we stop learning and growing do we not ossify, stagnate, and become forever captives of our past? The schools of our culture do not yet regard continued adult learning as vital; schools are for the young.

Stifling Schools

In the book, *Teaching as a Subversive Activity*, there is an important list of stifling attitudes that our culture and our schools engender:*

—Passive acceptance of ideas is a more desirable response than active criticism.

—Discovering knowledge is beyond the power of students and is, in any case, none of their business.

—Recall is the highest form of intellectual achievement, and the collecting of unrelated "facts" is the goal of education.

—The voice of authority is to be trusted and valued more than independent judgment.

—One's own ideas and those of one's classmates are inconsequential.

—Feelings are irrelevant in education.

—There is always a single unambiguous right answer to a question.

—English is not history, and history is not science, and science is not art, and art is not music; and art and music are minor subjects while English, history, and science are major subjects; and a subject is something you "take" and, when you have taken it, you have "had" it, and if you have "had" it, you are immune and need not take it again (the vaccination theory of education).

A thoughtful review of this list might reveal the same hidden attitudes in the church's subsystem of education. For although the church has traditionally addressed itself to education, it has usually regarded itself—or been regarded—as the voice of authority that tells its students the "facts" which they are faithfully to memorize and regurgitate. If you can recite the Lord's Prayer and the Apostles' Creed you are religiously educated!

Furthermore, religious education traditionally has been for the young. Once children have been through Sunday school and confirmation or baptism classes they have "had" it—as indeed they have!

Education as Process

Our word *education* comes from the Latin root *educare*, "to lead forth." Education is part of growth. It is not the acquisition of utilitarian skills and knowledge, but a leading forth to newness. It is the enlargement of self.

And the self that is alive is always enlarging. Therefore, just as the moralizing system is concerned with process, so the learning-growth subsystem is concerned with a never-ending enterprise that necessarily involves *all* its members in a comprehensive experience of learning and growth throughout their entire life.

This process does not involve just religion in the narrowest sense. It encompasses the learning-growth potential of the whole person. For, as we have seen, the church system is involved with the totality of being. In this sense, religious education cannot be narrow or fragmented but must embrace all areas of human beings and behaving.

The Sustaining-Maintaining Subsystem

An achievement-oriented society tends to value external visible accomplishment. It tends to devalue the invisible effort needed to keep the system going.

Keeping the System Going

In many homes today, for example, every member of the family works outside the home. That is important work—out there producing, serving, earning. But what about the meals, dishes, laundry, cleaning, yard work, car maintenance, bill

paying, faucet fixing? Is all that work just of nuisance value?
I think not.

No system can function without maintenance. There may
be little visibility, less glory, and even no pay. But without
maintenance the system will grind to a halt. In the church
system we can quickly think of janitors, secretaries, and ushers
—all the people who maintain yards and buildings, canvass
the membership, provide transportation, make telephone calls.
Odd jobs, perhaps, but they are essential jobs.

The importance of maintenance is illustrated in time studies
of human service organizations. Only 60 percent of pro-
fessional-staff time is given to direct services. Where does the
other 40 percent go? To maintenance functions. No system
can program its functions without a major allocation to maintenance.

As Paul suggests in 1 Corinthians, chapter 12, this subsystem and its members must be given recognition, appreciation, even glory, by the other parts and members of the church
system. The church needs and depends on a subsystem for
maintenance of the whole.

Nourishing the Members

The other dimension of this subsystem is the sustaining and
maintaining of the membership. We all need human relations
that maintain, sustain, restrain, correct, and nourish us.
Church people need that too.

We tend to look all too intently at what the church is ac-
complishing out there, in a visible way. But for a church
system to accomplish—out there—it must also nourish those
within.

Without nourishment the members starve and grow weak.
And weakness in its members can lead to a weak church
system. When members are strong and able, they make the
system vigorous.

The Reparative Subsystem

Life is filled with stress. Stress, when we cannot cope with
it, becomes crisis. And life crisis can become a clinical problem if there is no effective system to respond to the crisis.

Systemic Repair

How we cope with periodic and episodic dysfunction, disequilibrium, and disability is related to the ability of our system to effect repair. I use the term *repair* or *reparation* here deliberately in order to avoid too clinical an overtone. All of us experience being torn apart in our lives. At such times we may need help in "putting it all together" again. One partner in an effective marriage can nurse, nourish, and help repair the other partner. A family can absorb and help reintegrate one of its members who is distraught or torn. The people in a neighborhood can help a neighbor family weather a crisis of unemployment or accident.*

Similarly the church needs a subsystem that can respond to stress and crisis situations in the life of its membership. It needs eyes and ears alert to human need, and hands and hearts geared to ministry where need exists.

Church and Community

Human needs are of many kinds. They are individual and social. They are physical and spiritual. They are psychological and material. In meeting them the reparative subsystem provides another link between church and community.

The reparative subsystem can provide group contact, social relations, for persons who are exposed to particular life stresses that make them emotionally vulnerable. Through the life and activity of church-sponsored groups a vital contribution can be made to sustaining and revitalizing such persons. Churches address themselves to this need through groups for adolescents, old people, middle-aged adults, divorcées, single persons, people in the armed forces. Such groups are not for therapy as such; they simply provide an opportunity for human contact and for relating to other people. They enhance socialization among people who may be relatively isolated and in need of structured means for participating in supportive fellowship.

Churches can also provide concrete material and human assistance to people in the midst of specific life crises. It is to be expected that in the ordinary course of events people will experience unsettling stresses. It is not neurotic to go through

emotional upheavals or to find coping difficult at these times.
Here churches are uniquely equipped to help people cope and
to live through crises. Such help is provided in natural
human ways. The family moving to a strange city may receive advice and assistance through the church during their
relocation. The family that has suffered a death can find
support and comfort in time of bereavement. Some churches
sponsor widow-to-widow programs of personal support. The
family that is unemployed, burned or flooded out of their
home, or overwhelmed by medical catastrophe can obtain
shelter, food, clothing, and human concern.

These are all common predicaments of life. They are ordinary, not extraordinary. Yet it is in these common life
crises that the attendant emotional stress will either become
debilitating or be dealt with—depending upon the resources
available during the crisis to those who are stricken. The
church can provide such resources.

Finally, in the area of social concerns the church may lend
verbal and material public support; supply monies; provide
clerical and lay leadership, volunteers and facilities to programs aimed at redressing those social problems in the community which are helping to generate stress and crisis.
Churches may collaborate in the establishment and operation
of interracial dialogue programs, preschool education, nursery
schools for working mothers, alcohol and drug education, sex
education, open housing programs, health and education services for migrant workers.

The reparative subsystem makes the church available and
responsive to human needs. It assists in the repair and
binding-up of the hurt, the broken, and the needy. The
healthy system, as we have seen, is semipermeable, facilitating
integration and involvement and interaction between congregation and community.

Subsystems and the System

Each subsystem is part of the total system. Each subsystem
has its place and function within the larger system. Each
supports the other. The church as living system is effective

when it is proclaiming, symbolizing, moralizing and fostering morality, teaching and facilitating growth, sustaining itself and its members, and providing help and healing in time of stress and crisis. It is most effective when its efforts in all these areas are mutually reinforcing.

And, in turn, it is through its several subsystems working separately and together that the church as a whole relates to the community. In this sense the church is itself a subsystem of the larger community system. It is not a closed system sufficient unto itself. It is semipermeable, having connecting links both with the lives of its individual members and—through its subsystems—with the life of the community in which those lives are lived. The pastor needs to be aware of how the functioning of the church relates to the functioning of the larger community. The pastor's role in the church is not directed exclusively to the church but to enabling the lives of all the members for their inevitable participation in the community.

5. The Shepherd of the Church System

> Till I come, give attendance to reading, to exhortation, to doctrine. Neglect not the gift that is in thee, which was given thee by prophecy, with the laying on of the hands of the presbytery.
>
> —1 Tim. 4:13–14 (AV)

Pastors today express confusion about their role. Not knowing who they *are*, they are also unclear about what they are to *do*. It is no secret—indeed no wonder—that ministers sometimes leave the ministry in large numbers.

The Pastoral Role

Who is the pastor? And what is the pastor's role? Is the pastor an administrator, fund-raiser, preacher, prophet, teacher? Is the pastor a parent-surrogate for surly children, an unrequited-love object for lonely people, a holy stand-in for worldly people? Should the pastor be a symbolic model of virtue, an underpaid salve to people's conscience, a virtuoso demagogue of mustard-seed faith, or simply the person next door who is doing his or her thing in community betterment?

These are some of the questions that arise out of the current role confusion. The answer has to be: All or none of the above!

Functional Losses

We have already seen how in present times, in our century, there has been a notable loss in the *doing* functions of the church. There has also been a comparable attrition in terms of the pastoral role.

In the prototype village-church the pastor was often the most educated person around, a leader of the community.

48

The minister was the preacher, teacher, community services coordinator, health and welfare consultant, social reformer and community organizer, as well as psychotherapist to all. As the church of old served many community needs, so the pastor filled many pastoral roles.

Today as I meet with pastors I often hear the complaint: "But I am asked to fill so many roles. I can't do them all." Although there is some legitimacy in the complaint about multiple demands, I believe it obscures the more fundamental issue involved in function loss. For pastors also express their feelings of worthlessness, ineffectiveness, and lack of a legitimate identity and function. In a word, pastors have lost their status. Their role has been diminished. And with that comes demoralization. Loss has its emotional consequences.

The problem today is not that the pastor has too many roles, for pastors have always filled many roles. The problem is rather that many of the traditional pastoral roles have been secularized and taken over by public and private specialists in education, health, welfare, psychotherapy, social action, and community organization. Thus pastors find themselves in an ambiguous situation, competing with secular specialists— people who in specific areas at least may have more education, training, sanction, and support—for the specialist roles that the pastors used to perform.*

Dysfunctional Responses

I have observed two types of pastoral reactions to this functional loss. Both tend to be dysfunctional, even detrimental.

First, there is the generalist response. This is the reaction of the pastor who tries to retain some minimal expertise in everything and do at least a little bit of everything. This type of pastor is determined to "try harder." But as the Amish say, "the faster one goes the behinder one gets." Pastors who do it all themselves soon tire—"If only I had the time."

The second reaction is the specialist response. This is the reaction of the pastor who does not try to compete with the various secular specialists but instead picks out a specialty role. Often pastors concentrate on the preaching role. They

perform other functions only grudgingly and get little satisfaction from them. They see their identity as proclaimer and
find their satisfaction in sermon preparation and presentation.
The problem here is that subsystems of the church other
than the proclaiming subsystem begin to atrophy; they fail to
be supportive of, reciprocal to, the preaching.

Both these dysfunctional reactions tend to focus mainly on
what the pastor *does*. From a systems point of view, the
generalist response and the specialist response both involve
an inadequate definition of the pastoral role. For in relation
to the church as a system, the role of the pastor is primarily to
care for the subsystems that comprise the system of the
church. Thus the pastoral role is not so much a matter of
what the *pastor* does, as what the pastor enables the *system*,
operating in and through its subsystems, to accomplish. At
stake is the question of who the pastor *is*.

Pastoral Identity

I see the pastor as essentially a shepherd of systems. The
pastor functions to nurture and guide the subsystems of the
church. The pastoral role is determined by the pastor's systemic identity. For pastors, doing and being go together.
And pastoral care is care of the *church* as a living system.

I have found it illuminating to think of pastoral role in
terms of professional identity, with other professionals, such as
that of the medical doctor, affording a helpful analogy. The
pastor's being and doing is not unlike that of the physician, for
both have a common ancestry.

The Priest-Physician

In primitive society the healer was the shaman or witch
doctor, the priest-physician. Mind and body were one. Sin
was sickness, and sickness was sin. The shaman was simultaneously the healer of both spirit and body. Through the
performance of healing acts and rituals the spiritual problem
was resolved and the body healed. The effectiveness of the
shaman depended not on what one did but on who one was.

We have all seen the parent who kisses the cut finger of a

child to "make it well." I have kissed hurt fingers myself. The parent is an effective "healer" because of being that child's parent, not because of any therapeutic potency inherent in the kissing of fingers.

As societies became more complex the shaman's role became more complex. Illness came to be defined less as a personal spiritual problem and more as a natural phenomenon. Shamans were then defined by their technical skills, what they could do rather than who they were. As this trend progressed the spiritual functions and the technical functions of the shaman came to be separated into two divergent professional roles: the priest role and the physician role. Healing was likewise separated into two distinct components: spiritual healing of the person (soul) and technical healing of the pathology (body).

But this kind of separation is misleading. After all, certain aspects of the priestly function do not depend on personal skills and techniques, but on the person's role as an expression of identity. Think, for instance, of sacramental rituals, baptisms, confessionals, last rites. What is at issue in such rites is not technical competence. Indeed, the priest is regarded as effective simply because of who he or she is, namely, a priest.

By contrast, we tend to evaluate a physician not on the basis of role-identity, but in terms of technical competence. Yet it must be obvious that this contrast too is a distortion; for the priest (or minister, or rabbi) is expected to acquire competency in a variety of human helping and ministering skills, and conversely a physician's effectiveness is often more dependent on who he or she is than on technical performance. Both priest and physician are concerned with the healing of the individual, the person, and the professional healing role continues to retain some combination of both who the healer is and what the healer can do.

Here being and doing are not mutually exclusive but overlapping. They play complementary roles in the role of the professional person. Priest and physician are both concerned with the wholeness of persons, none of whom can be arbitrarily divided into physiological and psychological parts.

The priest who perceives his or her task solely as the saving of souls fails to see and serve the emotional, social, and physical needs of the parishioner. Likewise, the physician who perceives the medical task solely in terms of restoration of physiological function ignores the emotional, social, and spiritual needs of the patient.

This is why priest and physician often—to good effect—consult with each other. People do not have just spiritual problems or just physical problems. Rather they have a "problem in living." Birth control, a mentally retarded child, a terminal illness—these are problems in living that involve a person totally, in terms of spiritual attitude and feeling as well as medical status and symptoms.

There is an aphorism attributed to Oliver Wendell Holmes: "The physician's task is to cure rarely, relieve often, and comfort always." This highlights the overlapping role of priest and physician, in that both professionals deal with people who come with problems of living for which there is "rarely" a uniquely spiritual or medical "cure." Both priest and physician try rather to "comfort always" and "relieve often." But whether a person will seek a priest or a physician for the needed comfort and relief may be largely a matter of arbitrary and artificial choice. The person whose problem in living is expressed in terms of such symptoms as anxiety, guilt, or feeling bad about himself or herself may seek out the services of a priest. Another person whose identical problem in living is expressed in terms of such symptoms as chronic pain, stomach upset, or dysmenorrhea may seek out the services of a physician. But the priest who dismisses the person with a prayer and the physician who dismisses the person with a pill may equally have ignored the true needs of the person.

Arthur Shapiro makes an interesting observation: only in the past fifty years has the physician had much in the way of specific medicines or techniques to offer the patient; yet the physician has been significantly helping patients for centuries.* The curative factor throughout history has been in the personal relationship between patient and physician. And for this reason priests, ministers, rabbis, teachers, even philosophers and faith healers today can often "help" people more than the physician. As Peabody stated in his famous Harvard lecture: "The treatment of disease may be entirely impersonal . . . but the care of the patient must be completely personal. . . . The secret of the care of the patient is in caring for the patient."*

In a similar vein Erik Erikson insists that: "Clinical arts and sciences, while employing the scientific method, are not defined by it or limited by it. . . . The healer is committed to a highest good, the preservation of life and the furtherance of well-being."†

The role of the priest and the role of the physician are obviously overlapping roles when it comes to caring for people in distress. To separate the roles, to remove the overlapping would not only be detrimental; it is in fact impossible. The roles cohere as surely as the person to be served is not fragmented but a total spiritual-physical being.

Pastors need not shrink from such a dual—multiple—role. The system—both of the individual and of the church—is such that such multiple and overlapping roles are inevitable. As the pastor's role is that of "healing" in the broadest sense— a "caring" role—so pastoral care in the life of the church must be the healing of the church system. Pastoral care, by any name, cannot ignore the systems approach.

The Pastor as Symbol

A living system, as we have seen, functions to bestow and nurture identity. The church system does this not only for the members but for the minister as well, not least of all as a part of the symbolizing function.

Who you are, as pastor, may be seen in the symbolic nature of your position. That symbolic significance is critical to the performance of what you *do*. Once again, doing and being go hand in hand.

The Person as Symbolic

Consider the fact that small children tend to see their parents as omniscient, omnipotent, and omnipresent—even though they cannot pronounce these big words. "My Dad can do anything." "My Mom knows everything." "My folks are always here." When Freud first observed this phenomenon, he noted that children expressed disappointment, frustration, anger, and even rage whenever they experienced their parents as less than omniscient, omnipotent, and omnipresent.

In *The Future of an Illusion*, Freud postulated that to compensate for the inevitable failure of our parents to meet these childish expectations we create a Heavenly Parent, a God who is supremely omniscient, omnipotent, and omnipresent.* We need not accept Freud's postulate that God is merely a projection to meet our childhood disappointment. But his observations of our childhood feelings are accurate. The projection of the phantasized perfect Parent is an observed reality: it is clearly seen with respect to the role of the professional.

There are three historic professions: the law, the ministry, and medicine. It has long been held in the common-law tradition that people have the inalienable right of access to and services of a lawyer, a minister, or a doctor. In any time of need, no matter when or where—and irrespective of ability to pay—every person has the right to request and to have a lawyer, a minister, or a doctor. In other words the professional, at least in our fantasy, is omnipresent.

The professional is also omniscient. We actually expect the lawyer, the minister, or the doctor to be able to meet our need, solve our problem, help us, and care for us. In times of crisis we do not question their professional competence; we count on it. We assume their skill and knowledge.

Finally, the professional is seen as omnipotent. We are not told to exercise our own judgments, capacities, or competence. We are to trust rather in the power of the professional. We place our dilemma, indeed our destiny, in the hands of the doctor, the minister, the lawyer.

Now of course I am speaking of the irrational fantasy and impulse within ourselves. Yet these basic impulses play an important role, for during times of crisis and stress we all tend to regress. That is, we experience ourselves in terms of basic feelings of childhood. We feel threatened, helpless, fearful.

Our adult self tends to melt away, and we may feel that old primordial sense out of whose depths we cry: "Mommy, Daddy, where are you—help me." The *thoughts* may not emerge that explicitly, but our feelings and actions reflect the depth of our regressive anguish. At that point, when we seek help from a lawyer, a minister, or a doctor, we are likely to relate to that professional in terms of our childhood need for a succorer Parent-God figure.

Some years ago I cut my arm in an accident. As I was being rushed to the hospital my friend noticed that my face had turned an ashen gray. He told me about it. I calmly replied that as a trained psychiatrist I was well aware of the fact that I was experiencing traumatic anxiety and that I had a hyperventilation syndrome. What is interesting here is that while I knew this about myself, and articulated it too, my self-knowledge left me still ashen gray! On arrival at the hospital, however, the skilled and calm physician reassured me and relieved my anxiety. In the excellent care offered by this specialist I relaxed. I was secure in his knowledge and power. When I awoke after the successful operation I was gently tucked into bed by a soothing Mother-Angel, whom I felt was the most wonderful caring person in the world—she would let nothing hurtful happen to me. Alas, by noontime my anesthesia had worn off and I found my minor surgery most minor. I was up and ready to go home under full self-control. Only then did I discover that my Mother-Angel was a frumpy-grumpy nurse, and that my marvelous surgeon was a nervous young man in his first year of residency!

So much for regressive fantasies! But please note the symbolic role played by these two helping people. They not only assuaged my crisis, they allowed me to *let* them help me!

Symbols of the System

Thus the symbolic role enables the professional to carry out the technical tasks. When a parishioner comes to confess sins and seek absolution the transaction depends primarily on the symbolic role of the priest or pastor. Both participants have prior expectations regarding the symbolic function, and the symbol facilitates the action.

I attended court one day when a bewildered prisoner was in the dock. The judge solemnly intoned: "You will now receive your sentence. Please stand and face the court." The confused prisoner shuffled to his feet and turned curiously toward the gallery of spectators. Then the judge sternly announced: "Sir, you face *me!* *I* am the court!" Of course everyone laughed, including the judge. But the point was well made. The bench, the robe, the flag, the rail, the dock, the gavel—all betoken the system of the law. But the judge, in his person, was the living symbol of that legal system.

Even so, I see the church as a symbolic system in which the person of pastor is the living symbol of that system. The pastor is the symbol of both the human parent and the Heavenly Parent. This symbolic role is a two-edged sword. On the positive side, it affords the pastor a fulcrum upon which to gain leverage to change people and systems. On the negative side, it can evoke distorted emotional responses from parishioners who may hold unrealistic expectations, hopes, and fantasies about the pastor; indeed, it may even evoke in the pastor unrealistic self-perceptions. When I speak of the symbolic role, I am speaking primarily of the *realistic* images and expectations evoked by the pastor. However, I am not unaware of the attendant perceptual distortions which can and do occur, and I mean to deal with them in chapter 7.

In summary, *who we are* is reciprocal to *what we do.* The symbolic role of the pastor is a vital attribute of the pastoral calling. In that symbolic role the pastor is entrusted with particular needs of precious human beings. It is important that the pastor neither deprecate the symbolic role nor take unfair or abusive advantage of it. Rather, a pastor is called to a "high calling," to live out the role with dignity, restraint, and respect both for oneself and for one's people. Where "much has been given"—and the sacred symbolic role of pastor is much indeed—a high degree of faithfulness is required on the part of the trustee.

6. System Functions of the Shepherd

> We will lovingly follow the truth at all times—speaking truly, dealing truly, living truly—and so become more and more in every way like Christ who is the Head of his body, the church. Under his direction the whole body is fitted together perfectly, and each part in its own special way helps the other parts, so that the whole body is healthy and growing and full of love.
>
> —Eph. 4:15-16 (LB)

This passage from Ephesians suggests some important insights for our consideration: Christ is the head or leader of the church. The pastor is the symbolic representation of Christ. For any system to function there must be a leader. In the living system of the church the pastor is that leader. The function of the leader is to "direct the whole body" to the end that the parts mesh with one another and exercise mutual care and help.

The Pastor as Leader

We have seen already in chapter 3 that the provision of leadership is one of the primary functions of the strong and healthy church system. The leader's function is that of enabler. The leader in the system enables each part to function to help every other part, so that in reciprocal interaction and mutuality—in communion—the whole body grows. Within the church system this results in an important paradox: the most effective leader—the best pastor—will become increasingly less visible as the functioning of the system becomes more effective and manifest. This is because the leader is a part of, not apart *from*, the whole system.

The Leader and the System

The functions of the leader must be seen in terms of the dynamics of the system as such. In chapter 1 we mentioned three dynamic principles of a living system. The principles of holism, synergy, and isomorphism help to clarify—and determine—the systemic functions of the leader.

Consequently the leader does not tell the system what to do. The leader simply performs a special part, namely, the leader's part—that of enabling the system to be self-generative. This is in accord with the principle of holism, whereby group identity, the identity of the system, is different from and greater than that of any of its parts (including the leader).

As part of the system, the leader is also subject to the principle of synergy. That is, the leader is involved in interaction with all other members of the system. The leader whose actions are congruent with the goals of the system will potentiate the actions of all other members, and they in turn will potentiate the action of the leader. But if the leader acts in ways that fail to potentiate the others, the leader will in turn be blocked by the system. This is not to say that the leader is a passive pawn. It is to suggest that a leader can lead only to the extent that such leadership potentiates the whole system. There is a reciprocity of endeavor, support, influence, and growth between the leader and the system.

The principle of isomorphism also applies in the relationship between the leader and the system. That means that the leader while having a unique identity and function, also shares an identity and purpose which are those of the system. Here again there is a dialectical tension between individual identity and system identity. The leader is not the system. The system is not the leader. But neither is what it is without the other, and because of the other the two have a remarkable commonality of shape and function. They share common goals.

Developmental Stages

Because of the intricate and unending interaction between the leader and the system the functions of the leader inevitably reflect the different stages of system development. At each level of development the relationship between the leader and the system is different. The leader must expect the functions of leadership to be modified as the system matures. The different stages may be pictured in terms of a movement from storming to forming to norming to performing, as diagrammed on page 61.

Stage 1. Storming

In this stage we have a group of individuals who are not yet systemically related to each other except on an ad hoc basis. The leader is off to one side. The leader may call the group together and even get them to engage in joint work, study, or worship on a limited basis at fixed times and places. But the members are held together only by dint of the leader's effort.

Such an arrangement is not yet a true system, but only a pseudosystem. It does not yet manifest the properties of a living system—holism, open synergy, and isomorphism. The leader functions to bring individuals together—with a view toward the engendering of systemic interaction.

Stage 2. Forming

In this stage initial steps have been taken toward the formation of a system. Something new is coming into being. There is a shared common identity; there are shared goals. The leader is still perceived mainly as an outsider; in the movement from Stage 1 to Stage 2 the leader is usually outside the group, even if this is not always consciously recognized by all concerned.

The dominant motif here in Stage 2 is similarity: "We are alike; we are all the same." For this reason the leader cannot be recognized as such—cannot be acknowledged as different any more than any other member can be acknowledged as being different. Accordingly the leader is either deliberately excluded from the group, or is covertly reduced from a unique leadership role to the common role of being "one of us." This stage is therefore deceptive, for on the surface it appears as if this is a mature group, the superficial appearance being the consequence of a common assent to certain shared arrangements and purposes. The leader functions to intensify and deepen the levels of interaction and reciprocity.

Stage 3. Norming

In this stage the problems inherent in Stage 2 clearly emerge. The shared identity and common purpose require each member to contribute in the same way. This blocks individuality. As the group gets down to work there is a heightened tension between individual and group fulfillment and achievement. Persons who protest against the tyranny of the group and assert their individual identity will be labelled as deviants. They may begin to withdraw from the group in order to protect their individual identity; or the group may begin to exclude the deviants in order to protect the group identity. The leader is vulnerable at this stage, because if one asserts leadership one will be seen as threatening the group identity.

This stage of norming is often taken to represent an undesirable reaction. It is valued negatively. Leaders and groups may attempt to regress to Stage 2. From a systems point of view, however, Stage 3 is a critical stage in system development. It is an indispensable growth phase that is vital for progress toward a mature system. The leader functions to identify the tension, confront the conflict, and facilitate the resultant growth within self and others.

Stage 4. Performing

In this stage the system achieves "resolution" of the conflict between individual identity and system identity—not that the tension is done away, but it is accepted as inevitable and fruitful. There is a mutual recognition of and commitment to system identity, and at the same time a mutual recognition of and commitment to each individual's unique identity and personal contribution to the system and its functioning.

Finally the leader is recognized as a member of the system, a full-fledged partner in the common enterprise. The leader shares in the common system identity, with the resultant gain —not loss—in individual identity. The leader is acknowledged as leader, and as leader makes a unique contribution to the system. Not least in this contribution is the leader's personal and paradigmatic handling of the identity conflict in a creative way.

STAGES OF SYSTEM DEVELOPMENT

Stage 1. Storming
Amorphous, unstructured, individually autonomous behavior. Systemic behavior generated only by the leader.

individuals   leader

Stage 2. Forming
Development of a common identity and unity. Individual autonomy subverted in the cause of group cohesion and group identity, the development of a "group mind" and "group will." The leader is separate from the system but allowed to relate to it.

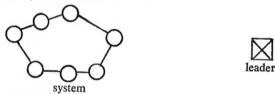

system   leader

Stage 3. Norming
Members experiencing anxiety over threatened loss of individual identity and autonomy. Individuals distancing themselves from the group. The leader is caught in the same tension between identification with the system and assertion of one's unique leadership role.

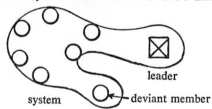

leader

system   deviant member

Stage 4. Performing
Dialectical tension between individual identity and system identity, between commitment to self and to the system. The leader role is found to be only one example of the general tension shared by all.

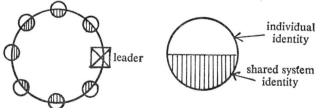

leader   individual identity

shared system identity

System Development in the Church

In the church a Stage 1 system may be characterized by the charismatic pastor who pulls a group of people together and holds them together through dynamic personal leadership. The leader assumes total responsibility for the operation of the system. Indeed, the system will not function without the leader.

A Stage 2 system is not as dependent on the pastor, so long as the pastor is in complete accord with the church system. However, the pastor will find difficulty in leading this church in the direction of change, nor will this church allow the pastor to lead. New members will be welcome if they fit into the preestablished system, but dissidents will not be tolerated. This church may grow in numbers, but remains in an unstable state that can be easily rocked by any threatened change from within or without.

A Stage 3 system occurs when the pastor (or church) does not recognize the necessary tension between individual and group identity. The nature and value of such tension is not openly and explicitly resolved. There is a perpetual tug-of-war between member and group. This is a church in conflict.

Stage 4 is what I term a mature living systems church. Here the pastor is personally creative in resolving for and with others the dynamic tensions that go with systemic interaction.

The Leader's Contribution

The one most critical variable for system function is the quality of leadership. Every leader gets the system he or she deserves. And every system gets the leader it deserves. So the system leader must always keep a watchful eye on leadership.

The shepherd of the system must constantly be asking questions: Is my leadership resulting in desired system function? If not, how can I use my leadership to effect desired change?

You, the pastor, cannot be responsible *for* the system—you can only be responsible *for* yourself. However, you must be responsible *to* the system.

I am reminded of that ancient prayer of serenity which in one of its versions goes like this: "God grant me the courage to change the things I can, the serenity to accept what I cannot change, and the wisdom to know the difference." There are always aspects of a system that cannot be changed. These must be clearly defined. Then one must address the task of changing what *is* changeable in the system.

System leadership is not a matter of passivity, nor yet of consensus. It requires rather an active unique contribution, the contribution of one living member in a dynamic and integrated living system. That contribution can be further specified in terms of seven discrete functions.

Seven Leadership Functions

The Symbolizing Function

Every living system has an identity which is expressed through shared values and goals. These values and goals are embodied in symbols that serve as the constant standard of reference. The pastor, by virtue of the pastoral office itself, is a major symbol of the church system. The pastor must provide a continuing affirmation of the group identity, its purposes, its values, and its goals.

The minister's very presence carries with it an implicit message. The pastor is a systemic reminder of what the system is. In therapy group meetings there is a lot of chatter at the beginning of each session until the group leader enters—then the group falls into quiet. Finally someone says: "Well, I guess we have to get down to work." Thus the entrance of the leader symbolizes the purpose of the group, and to that symbol the group responds.

The pastor may make his or her symbolic function explicit. One may speak to the purposes, values, and commitments of the system. One may explicitly remind the system, or reaffirm the system.

The pastor does not *tell* the system what its identity is. The pastor does not *create* definitions for the system. Rather the pastor consistently *recalls* for the system what the system has created.

In effect the pastor says: "Let me refresh our memories— we agreed to come together and commit ourselves to. . . ." In this symbolizing function the pastor continually stands as a reminder of the system commitment. The pastor does not operate from outside the system. The pastor does not speak *to* the system. Rather the symbolizing is done *for* the system, from *within*. The pastor calls the system to self-awareness.

The Being Function

Here the pastor affirms the individual identity of each member of the system. Whereas in the symbolizing role it is the group identity, the universal identity, that is affirmed, in the being role the pastor affirms himself or herself as a unique person, thereby affirming each individual member of the system as a unique person.

It is a mistake to assume that in the symbolic role the pastor must attempt to be a paragon of virtue. That is not only impossible; it is also inappropriate—for the very reason that in the symbolic proclamation the pastor is *not* pointing to himself or herself. The point of symbolic reference is not oneself but the Lord, not the leader/member of the body, but the Head of the whole body. The pastor is not a model, but a symbol.

This understanding of the symbolizing functions enables the being function. It frees the pastor to *be* a person.* One need not try to hide one's imperfections. One need not fear making mistakes. One need not attempt to come up with perfect answers all the time. One need not be able to solve every problem.

As no member of a system is alone complete and perfect, so the pastor is not complete as an individual. On the contrary, the pastor can present himself or herself as simply one member, with assets and limitations, who can and will contribute to the whole. Wherever one is free to be oneself that freedom is liberating for others. The pastor who in freedom acts to be himself or herself sets the standard for all members to be free to be themselves. The pastor is not, cannot, and does not strive to be perfect, nor to set a goal of perfection for others, but rather sets a standard of honest integrity. Pastors strive simply to be themselves, and thereby make their contribution out of their own limited resources. In turn, all other members can be themselves, and can contribute from their limited re-

sources. Pastors who can accept limited humanity in themselves enable others toward similar self-acceptance.

The Sharing Function

The pastor is *not* the system. The pastor is *part* of the
system. In consequence the pastor shares with the system.
There is much to be shared.

First of all, one must share one's narcissism. The pastor
must give up the desire always to be center stage, the chief
benefactor of the rewards. If the system is effective, its accomplishments are those of the total system, not of the pastor
alone. This means that the pastor must give up the very real
satisfaction of pointing to "what *I* accomplished." One must
find one's narcissistic reward indirectly through seeing the
accomplishment of a *system* in which one's own role is *not*
seen. In a family, the father who refuses to share the lime-
light may engage only in actions that directly reward himself.
The eminent politician or businessman is frequently such a
father: his children are often failures in life. In contrast, the
father who potentiates his children may receive no *direct*
recognition, but in the end have the satisfaction of seeing his
children succeed.

Second, the pastor must share responsibility. The pastor
who tries to hang onto all the reins of responsibility is often
left holding them all himself: the system as such will not act
responsibly.

Third, the pastor must share authority. Responsibility
without any commensurate authority to make the necessary
decisions is empty.

Fourth, one must share control. The pastor who attempts
to control everything controls nothing. In a family system the
mother may perceive herself as being in control—but only
because the family allows her that self-deception. In any family system there is a carefully regulated set of balances and
interactions. No one controls the family unless the family
system allows it. Just so in the church system, a pastor may
have control, but if he or she does, it is only because the
church system allows it.

Is that necessarily bad? Yes, I think so. It really leaves

the pastor all alone. The pastor who alone shoulders the entire burden of responsibility-authority-control is extremely vulnerable to stress, crisis, or change. By depriving the system of its tools of strength that pastor loses out on the strength that the system could afford. That pastor also deprives the system of its potential for growth. In the family a parent who totally controls the child until the age of eighteen and then suddenly says, "All right, you are an adult—go take care of yourself," has deprived the child of the chance to learn, grow, and develop into maturity. In the same way, the pastor who refuses to share responsibility-authority-control will only rear a stunted and immature church that has no capacity to function as a mature living system.

The Intentionality Function

The mirror opposite of the controlling pastor is the pastor who is a caricature of the suffering servant. This pastor abdicates leadership altogether. Effective leaders are neither passive nor aggressively dominating. Rather they are synthetically active. They plan for the direction they wish to go, actively leading the system, and consciously choosing how and where they will interact with the system. Their functioning is not haphazard but intentional, not a matter of default but of decision.

The intentionality function is an active, not a reactive, dimension of leadership. It points to the maintainance of conscious intentions by which the leader sets daily priorities among the competing tasks clamoring for attention and effort. Beneath the bewildering diversity of demanding activities there is a deep underlying direction to one's work that gives it continuity and vision. This intentionality is a bulwark against complaints of futility, frustration, and powerlessness. One's leadership of the system is of one piece, coherent in its basic identity, defined intentions, and shared consciousness.

Edgar Mills describes this function quite succinctly:

> Intentionality is one basic work style. . . . It involves three levels: intentions such as planning, setting priorities, creating one's role, and mobilizing resources; vocation as a sense of

an underlying direction, movement, and meaning in one's
life; and the shared consciousness of the possibility of change,
taking the form of collaborative problem-solving. The central issue is to define areas of initiative consistent with one's
vocation and to enter into supportive relationships and shared
effort which will broaden and strengthen the intentional
base of one's ministry.*

Intentional behavior on the part of the pastor will potentiate
intentional behavior by members of the system. It will contribute to the system's sense of direction and purpose.

The Modeling and Risk-taking Function

There is an old ploy called the double bind. It goes like
this. "I know how I want you to act. However, I will not tell
you or show you. But when you don't act the way I want, I
will criticize you for not knowing and not acting the way I
want you to." Of course this leaves me smelling like a rose . . .
at least on first sniff! But there is a real problem here if the
leader refuses to show and tell. The system will experience a
feeling of inadequacy, ineptness, and stupidity. People will
shut up and withdraw rather than risk exposure as fools.
Where the leader will not speak the system will stutter.

There are two maxims which apply in this regard. The first
is: Don't ask people to do what you have not done first or are
not willing to do. The second is: Don't ask people to do
something without offering yourself as a trial model. To be a
leader is to stick out your neck.

By modeling of course I do not mean offering a perfect
example—far from it! Rather, I mean providing people with
a clear definition of what you are asking, and then giving them
an example of how it might be done—you offer yourself as an
example. You say, in effect: "Look, here is what we want to
do. I do not know precisely how to do it. But I would try it
this way. Criticize my attempt. See where I fail. Then see
if you can improve upon it." To offer yourself as an example
is not the same as making an example of yourself. It is not
public masochism. It is a matter of providing an innovative
model.

Such modeling involves risk. You take the first step. You

demonstrate your willingness to be exposed to observation and criticism. You afford the system an opportunity to see a member actually try out a solution. You do *not* offer yourself as the flawless model to be copied. But you do offer yourself as a model of willingness to experiment.

Again this freeing of the pastor to be himself or herself allows the other system members also to be themselves. It does not require that the pastor come up with a perfect solution, only that the pastor activate the system in its quest for an improved model for action.

The Limit-setting Function

I do not believe in the innate goodness of humankind. We all have within us the potential for both good and evil. Neither do 1 believe in the innate goodness of human systems. They too can work toward good or evil. Any human system, like any human being, can be capricious, chauvinistic, tyrannical, obtuse, and abusive. No human system, however idealistic its values and goals, when left to itself will necessarily operate toward the good of all. The frailty of humanity is reflected in the frailty of human systems. We see family systems that promote the health and growth of family members, but we also see family systems that stunt growth and destroy people.

Therefore, a critical function of the pastor is to stand watch over the functioning of the church system as well as continually to watch over each member. The pastor must be able and willing to set limits, never allowing the system to tyrannize over or sacrifice the individual member. As the vitality of the system is reflected in the vitality of each member, so the destruction of one member is destructive of the system as a whole. Systems—members—cannot be allowed to act destructively. Limits must be imposed and enforced.

Now limit-setting is *not* punishment. Punishment is a matter of getting even: you did something hurtful to me, so I will retaliate and do something equally hurtful to you. Rather, limit-setting is a matter of establishing boundaries of acceptable action. It is also a matter of maintaining those boundaries so that people must take the consequences of their actions. But limit-setting is more positive than negative. Discipline would be a better word for it. It implies a consistent demand for and reinforcement of right actions, and a refusal to accept or tolerate wrong actions. One who seeks the right will avoid the wrong. Thus the pastor, in the limit-setting function, must consistently reinforce the healthy behavior of the system and restrain the system from destructive action.

The Catalytic and Enabling Function

In a sense all seven functions of the system leader fall into this category. The leader is the enabler. However, we may speak of some specific tasks under this particular rubric.

The first is that of connector. The connecting task involves getting different subsystems linked together, so that they are able to see their common goals.

The second is that of mediator. The mediating function involves the tasks of conflict resolution, establishment of priorities, and the ordering of activities.

The third is that of facilitator. Facilitating involves the planning and organizing of subsystems so that they can begin to function.

Finally, there is the task of catalyst. The term *catalyst* is borrowed from the process of chemical reactions. You can mix chemical ingredients but get no reaction until you add just a pinch of the right catalyst to trigger the reaction. The catalyst overcomes the initial resistance, and once the chemical reaction is underway it proceeds from its own energy. In like manner, the pastor must supply that pinch of energy which is needed to overcome initial resistance, thus enabling the church system to engage in such interactions as will generate their own momentum.

To summarize, the function of the pastor as shepherd of the church system is to play his or her own unique role as a member or part of the whole system. The pastor's functions enable the system to be healthy, growing, and full of love. The system in turn then becomes the vehicle for health and growth of its individual members.

7. Distortions of the Shepherd

> The bishop, then, must be above reproach, the husband of
> only one wife, temperate, discreet, well-behaved, hospitable,
> qualified to teach.
>
> —1 Tim. 3:2 (MLB)

We have seen in chapter 4 the importance of the symbolizing function of the church system, and in chapter 5 how much
of that function is accomplished through the pastor, not so
much in virtue of specific pastoral skills as in virtue of the
pastoral office as such. Within the system as a whole the
symbolizing function of the system's shepherd is crucial, and
in a sense inevitable and automatic. The pastor's systemic
identity, as we have seen in chapter 5, gives central importance to the symbolic nature and symbolizing function of the
pastoral role. The person of the pastor becomes the living
symbol of the church as a symbolic system, and, as we have
seen in chapter 6, the symbolizing function may even rank
first among the functions of any leader.

Because this symbolic role places the pastor in an extremely
vulnerable and sensitive position, because it can not only facilitate pastoral effectiveness but also block it altogether, we
must examine potential distortions of the pastoral role. To
borrow a pair of terms from the therapist's handbook, we may
speak of the two major categories of distortion as those of
transference and countertransference.

During the course of a normal day's activities the pastor
meets people in a variety of settings involving personal need,
whether spiritual, physical, emotional, or social. In such settings, where needs are great, emotions run high. Unlike the
counseling setting, where the emotional context is relatively
controlled, the broader pastoral care setting may be right in
the middle of highly emotional social contexts that frequently

revolve about and play upon the symbolic role of the pastor. Thus the pastor, whether as object or as subject, is highly vulnerable to emotional distortions.

The parishioner's transference and the pastor's counter-transference may confuse and hurt both pastor and parishioner. Most importantly, these distortions and their management may augur the success or failure of pastoral care.

The Nature of Distortions

We observe in everyday life that people often misinterpret each other. Your view of me hardly accords with the reality of which I am aware—and vice versa. We often distort ordinary communications: "Once over lightly, please. I'm not reading you!" Sometimes these distortions are absurd, even hilarious. But it is no laughing matter when a wife misinterprets why her husband came home late, or when the soprano takes the choir director's suggestions as a personal insult. Such distortions of reality abound in the personal encounters of pastoral care, particularly so because the pastor is frequently dealing with emotionally charged situations, even acute crises. We may for our purposes mention three kinds of reality disturbances that commonly occur.

Transference Neurosis

Freud was the first to recognize and study the phenomenon of transference neurosis. He found that in his administration of psychoanalytic treatment the patient sometimes began to treat him *as if* he, the therapist, were some emotionally important figure from the patient's prior life. To Freud it seemed that the patient, loaded with disturbing ideas and feelings out of the past, simply "transferred" them onto the figure of the psychoanalyst. Almost like an electrical short circuit, the transfer took place as it were "through a false connection."* Feeling memories out of the past were applied directly to the current situation. The reoccurrence of childhood developmental conflicts and their transference in therapy to other persons and relationships reflected a renewed attempt to resolve those conflicts with a new figure.

Karl Menninger describes the phenomenon as follows: "the unrealistic roles or identities unconsciously ascribed to a therapist by a patient in the regression of the psychoanalytic treatment, and the patient's reactions to this representation derived from earlier experiences."* Transference neurosis is a one kind of *as if* distortion which easily develops within the intense emotional situation of psychotherapy. Some degree of transference neurosis is fairly common in many counseling relationships, and it is certainly not unknown in many of the highly charged encounters of pastoral care.

Interpersonal Distortions

Interpersonal distortions occur when we ignore the real characteristics of the other person and behave *as if* the relationship between us were quite different from what it actually is. It is almost as if during an interpersonal encounter *you* and *I* did not remain constant but became several different persons. During a consultation between a pastor and a deacon, for example, the relationship might shift from that of pastor-deacon to that of father-son, brother-sister, teacher-pupil, bully-coward, God-sinner, mother-infant, or boss-worker. The possibilities are many and the fluctuations between them varied.

There are many examples of such distortions in marriages. One husband was always suspicious of his wife when she talked to other men; it turned out that his mother had carried on illicit love affairs and that he was ascribing attitudes of his mother to his wife's behavior. In another case a wife became violently angry with her husband when he did not discipline the children; it turned out that he was truly and deeply concerned about their children, and that she had mistaken his leniency for the flagrant disinterest her own father had displayed.

Interpersonal distortions involve patterns of feeling and behavior in which *I* and *you* are experienced in terms of some *former* relationship so that the reality of the *present* situation is ignored or slighted. In counseling situations where these distortions can be pointed out they can also be used to therapeutic advantage. In less controlled situations in everyday life—and in pastoral care—where these distortions are overlooked, or even accepted at face value as reality and reacted to or mutually reciprocated, they may seriously obstruct any relationship.

Personality Distortions

A third type of distortion may be mentioned, the chronic personality distortions. These involve more fixed and habitual patterns of reaction. There is the person who is always angry or persistently passive, or eagerly erotic, or habitually humble, or durably dominant. All are types of characters who stand out because they cannot easily and quickly modulate their relationships and relating patterns according to the needs of the situation.

Such distortions usually become manifest in specific emotional encounters. For example, as a pastor I cannot accept my own dependent feelings and may therefore react with hostility to the old, the young, the helpless, or any others who try to lean upon me emotionally. Or as a pastor I fear my own anger and may therefore not be able to maintain firm discipline with the adolescents of the church. Or as a pastor I feel inadequate about myself as a human being and may therefore never be able to offer consolation in times of bereavement lest that accentuate my feelings of inadequacy.

Chronic personality distortions reflect unresolved conflicts that have become fixed in the personality and result in stereotyped responses that are not always adapted to the situation. The person involved is often seen as being insensitive to the feelings, reactions, and needs of others.

In the following discussion I shall, for the sake of simplicity, refer to all three types of reality distortion as transference or countertransference. These two broad terms can include the various kinds of distortion which may occur in any given situation. Some people think they apply only when the distortion has reference to feelings of dependency or sexuality and arises in the course of long-term intensive counseling. But this is not true. Reality distortions can involve any and all of our emotions, and they can occur in any setting or relationship. Indeed, it is precisely for this reason that some knowledge about them is crucial for the shepherd of the church system.

Transference in Pastoral Care

By virtue of the symbolic role which is so vital for effective pastoral functioning, the pastor is frequently placed in a position of symbolic conflict. Images of other provenance may be thrust upon the pastor in such a way as to warp the legitimate expectations of all concerned, and to unhinge their rootage in reality.

Images of God and Pastor

Parishioners may see the minister as an authority figure, a father or mother figure who is a stand-in for or representative of God. Seen in this light, the pastor is immediately the object of the universal ambivalence toward father authority and mother authority: on the one hand there is the feeling of veneration and respect; on the other hand there can be seething resentment, rebellion, and hostility. In some measure the ambivalence is probably to be found in every person. At times, however, it can lead to alignments which split the congregation. It can be acted out in church divisions where a positive response to authority leads some members to fanatic loyalty to the pastor, while a negative response to authority leads others to pull out and start a new church. In lesser form this same ambivalence feeds many of the petty rivalries that seem to flourish in most churches.*

Where people identify their pastor with God, the pastor is subject to the same distortions people make of God. It has been readily observed that children commonly model their anthropomorphic concepts of God on their conception of their own parents. It is only during adolescence, according to Piaget,† that children finally develop more abstract concepts of God that begin to approximate theological views of Deity. Unfortunately, many Christians never give up that anthropomorphic God of their childhood who remains a distortion of their own mother and father relationships.

These infantile God images ultimately affect the pastoral role. If God in the eyes of a parishioner is a mean old man, an aloof and disinterested mother, a violent and unpredictable parent, so too may be the pastor. On the other hand, the person who sees God as a kindly, all-giving, and ever-protective Beneficence may react with anger if the pastor does not fulfill all the associated expectations.

These undifferentiated identifications which indiscriminately connect parent, God, and pastor account for many of the feelings the parishioner experiences in relating to the pastor. Although the pastor may behave in quite innocuous fashion, he or she may be responded to as a vigorously condemning person. Rebellious members, particularly adolescents, may react to the authority of the pastor-God image by flouting their skepticism or by disdaining the conventions of church behavior. On the other hand, persons who from childhood on have learned to react to authority with a passive-submissive stance may acquiesce to all pastoral suggestions as if they were unquestionable commands. Indeed, they may react angrily if the pastor does *not* give them explicit guidance or specific commands to follow; they insist on being told what to do.

Sexual Transferences

Sexual transferences are common. The woman who overvalued and idealized her father may overestimate a male pastor and regard his wife as a rival. Such a woman may overpraise him, offer to do extra work for him, and defend his ideas against all detractors. By her actions she in effect hopes to win from her pastor the recognition and approval she has tried to win, sometimes in vain, from her own father. Unfortunately her expectations breed jealousy and anger if the pastor in turn does not give her the rewards she feels she merits. Similarly, a man may feel threatened by a woman pastor whom he perceives as a controlling mother figure.

Some people fear the expression of sexual impulses and tend to become defensive when they feel their own sexual impulses are being stimulated. Thus a minister may be surprised to discover that a warm, intense, personal approach evokes only a negative response from the parishioner who experiences such a pastoral approach as sexually stimulating, hence fearful. The pastor is well-advised, therefore, to refrain from any physical contacts or intimate gestures which may provoke unwanted sexual fantasies in the parishioner, and even frightened withdrawal.

Dependency Transferences

Grief affords another occasion for reality distortions. The person in grief usually experiences a sense of powerlessness about the situation, and anger over the attendant dependency.

The bereaved person may blame God for the sickness or death of a loved one, and accordingly project that anger onto the pastor. A young mother lost her son to a protracted bout with cancer. The pastor had kept an all-night vigil with the boy's parents, but when the child finally died the mother screamed in rage, cursed God, and beat on the pastor with her fists. She was infuriated by her own feelings of dependency and powerlessness.

For similar reasons elderly members of the congregation may react to the pastor in equally problematic fashion. On the one hand, they may resent the young man or woman who, as leader, they see replacing them or challenging their more mature wisdom. On the other hand they may truly wish to become childishly dependent on the pastor, who becomes for them a type of their own needed or missing grown child— watchful, concerned, solicitous for their welfare.

Indicators of Transference

It is important—and possible—for pastors to know when transference is occurring. Some indications of transference reaction may be briefly noted:

1. A person frequently requests individual attention;
2. A person reacts differently from others in the same group;
3. A person responds to routine pastoral work in an overly positive or overly negative way;

4. A person requests counseling in unusual places, times, or situations;
5. A person demands that the pastor act in his or her stead to resolve personal problems or make personal decisions;
6. A person fails to keep appointments or fulfill obligations;
7. A person is over-scrupulous in the performance of duties, especially those related to the pastor's work.

The recognition of transference is necessary if the pastor is to avoid playing into the parishioner's hands by accepting these distortions as real. Of course the pastor must also consider whether he or she is behaving in an inappropriately provocative or reactive fashion. In their work psychotherapists usually try to assume a neutral noncommittal role, one that is less likely to provoke distorted reactions. Pastors can in effect use somewhat the same approach by developing and maintaining a consistent sort of emotional stance with the congregation. If one remains consistent in dealing with persons and groups, one can readily recognize distortions when they occur. Each pastor has a unique personality and approach which can be used as a standard of measurement in assessing personal encounters and noting divergent reactions which may signal reality distortion.

Countertransference in Pastoral Care

Probably the most difficult task to learn in psychotherapy is how to handle one's own reactions to the emotional currents of intense interpersonal relationships. The same task confronts the pastor, and to no less a degree. After all, the pastor too, both socially and emotionally is intimately involved with the people with whom he or she works.

Dealing with the Pastor's Own Impulses

The pastor who is afraid of his or her own aggressive impulses may have difficulty in being firm, or in reacting with appropriate anger, or in using authority with judicious restraint but forthright conviction. The pastor who is afraid of his or her own sexuality may deny erotic feelings in situations where one should be aware that one is responding in a sexually provocative or reactive fashion. A male pastor, for example, may find a woman accusing him of improper advances. He protests his innocence. But had he recognized his own impulses from the outset he might have avoided playing into the mutual distortions of the sexual aspects involved in the pastoral relationship.

Countertransference distortions occur for the pastor when one attempts to solve one's own problems through the problems of the parishioner, or vicariously enjoys behavior in the parishioners which one feels one must deny in oneself. For example, a female pastor may find herself encouraging a young boy to extensively discuss his sexual fantasies with her, or a male pastor may find himself encouraging a husband to make major family decisions on his own, without considering the welfare or wishes of his wife and children.

Indicators of Countertransference

If pastors need to know when transference is occurring on the part of their parishioners, they need even more urgently to know when they themselves are experiencing countertransference. The following are some practical indications which may alert the pastor to countertransference problems:

1. I am careless in keeping appointments;
2. I experience repeated erotic or hostile feelings;
3. I notice that I am bored or inattentive during conversation;
4. I permit or encourage misbehavior;
5. I try to impress my parishioners;
6. I argue a lot;
7. I take sides prematurely in personal conflicts;
8. I prematurely reassure people to lessen my own anxiety;
9. I dream repeatedly about a parishioner;
10. I feel that the parishioner's welfare or need-fullfillment lies solely with me;
11. I behave differently toward one parishioner than toward others in the same group;
12. I make unusual appointments or behave in a manner that for me is unusual.

The pastor is certainly part of the parish reality and the pastoral reality, and needs to know when reality is being distorted—at any point—in order to be able to minister appropriately and function effectively. In this regard the pastor's own distortions, however natural or inevitable, need to be consciously addressed as surely as those of any parishioner. Leadership requires it.

Dealing with Distortions

The pastor is particularly subject to what Ernest Jones described as "the God complex."* Identification with God may result in feelings of omnipotence and omniscience, and belief in the magical power of one's own word to effect change. The pastor may be tempted to believe that he or she has all the answers to everyone's personal problems, or that people will be changed simply by the exercise of pastoral authority. In dealing with human problems however, it must be apparent that just saying the right words does not magically change people or their behavior.

Pastoral care, of course, is not purely passive, nondirective, and value-free. Quite the contrary! The pastor does exercise symbolic authority. The trick is to articulate and exercise that authority without "playing God"—which would clearly be a distortion of reality.

Unfortunately, much of the pastoral counseling literature in recent years has been heavily influenced by Carl Rogers, whose early ideas on nondirective counseling were widely adopted. His valuable technique has since been placed in broader perspective and seen to have a more limited application as pertaining to only one aspect of the counseling relationship. The value of the Rogerian emphasis should not be discarded: counselors can be of great assistance if they will help clients to understand their own problems and develop their own solutions. But nondirective counseling alone will not suffice. It would also be inauthentic for the shepherd of the church system.

The pastor is sought out precisely because he or she represents the reliable values, commitments, standards, and behavior patterns established by the church.* It is in the context of the church's commonly shared spiritual values and standards that pastoral care occurs. Crucial functions of the church system and its subsystems require that the system leader embody and articulate these values and standards. This does not mean, however, that it is enough for the pastor simply to reiterate the theology and morals of the church. The pastoral task lies in helping parishioners to deal with the conflicts and distortions of spiritual values in their own life and to resolve contradictions within their own behavioral and spiritual commitments. Predicaments of human conflict need to be dealt with by the humans involved, yet on the basis of and by the power of the church and according to the articulated standards of the church.

In pastoral care the pastor is offering help *as a pastor*, that is, in full and mutual recognition of a specific authority and responsibility, and by way of a specific type of interhuman relationship. It is inappropriate for the pastor to play psychiatrist. To do so would be to distort reality. The pastor who forsakes the pastoral role would be like the educator who treats his children as a schoolteacher instead of as a father. This is not to say that the father and the pastor cannot use their special skills to advantage, but only that their emotional roles and involvements must be as real persons and not as neutral functionaries. The shepherd's role is sadly distorted whether the pastor plays God or therapist!

A national study on mental health resources bears this out.† It was discovered that when people consult their pastor it is primarily with respect to problems of a personal nature— in their marriage, with their children, or with their relatives. Clergy counseling was preferred above other kinds of counseling because it makes less demand for introspection—interpersonal difficulties are seen in less psychological terms—and less implicit demand for change in the self, as compared to the counseling available through mental health agencies. Satisfied with the help they received, respondents reported appreciation of the clergy for their ability to provide comfort, advice, and reassurance. Most people were not seeking changes in themselves; they were simply looking for help in the resolution of interpersonal conflict.

As we have seen, there are many types of transference and countertransference. All are reality distortions. It should be apparent that the pastor faces these problems frequently. It is important to be able to recognize them in self as well as in others. It is usually *not* appropriate to attempt to interpret the distortions observed. This is true even for much psychotherapy, where the competent therapist carefully avoids making interpretations of the transference distortions because such interpretation is neither helpful nor relevant to the therapeutic task. Likewise in pastoral care, "wild interpretations" of the various distortions usually only muddy the picture and damage the pastoral relationship. What is needed more than interpretation is vigilance, to assure that the distortions are not taken for reality. Pastors can best preserve their pastoral role and protect themselves and their parishioners from the vicissitudes of transference and countertransference problems by keeping the relationship authentically pastoral and by focusing continually on the realities of the situation, the parishioner's real life, and the consciously available feelings which are related to these realities.

It is important to emphasize that the recognition of transference in the parishioner and countertransference in the pastor should not be an occasion for blame or condemnation. These distortions are the inevitable consequence of human encounter. Knowing that fact, and recognizing the distortions when they arise, can help the pastor maintain an unthreatened demeanor despite the distortions. Further, pastors may work constructively to modify their own distortions, and relate to people as real people despite blurred, warped, or shifting perceptions.

One thing they cannot do: they cannot allow distortions to pass unseen and unchallenged. Transference could vitiate pastoral effectiveness, and countertransference could mean betrayal of the pastoral role. A systemic view of the church—and of its shepherd—demands greater realism.

8. Shepherd to Shepherd

Share each other's troubles and problems, and so obey our Lord's command. If anyone thinks he is too great to stoop to this, he is fooling himself. He is really a nobody.

Let everyone be sure that he is doing his very best, for then he will have the personal satisfaction of work well done, and won't need to compare himself with someone else. Each of us must bear some faults and burdens of his own. For none of us is perfect!

—Galatians 6:2–5 (LB)

My goal in this book has been to share with fellow pastors something I have learned about human behavior and human systems, things which may be of value to them in the context of their parish ministry. Having written as one pastor to another, I shall conclude with some personal comments about being a shepherd of the flock.

The More and Less of Shepherding

A shepherd of systems is not sequestered but exposed, not isolated but involved. Enabling a system demands participation in the system. Of course it is easy to hide in the pulpit or the office, or even in a committee or a class. But you cannot hide from the church system as such if you are to be an effective pastor. Shepherding the system requires personal maturity and a renunciation of self-indulgence.

I want to share a discovery I have made about myself. When I first began my career as a psychotherapist I found myself in a quandary: I was one type of person in the therapy session, another with my professional colleagues, and yet another when I spoke publicly or preached in the church. Alas, patients who met me in the office or saw me talk to colleagues also showed up in the front row when I spoke. I know they were befuddled—I was too! But at least they didn't see me at home—where I had to meet yet another me.

But then I began to question: What nonsense is this? How can I speak to others about integrity in their life if I myself am not consistent? Must I not strive to be the same person at all times, whether in my office, with my colleagues, among friends and family, or in the pulpit?

Obviously, one does not behave identically in each situation, I thought, but there must be consistency of character. If I observe myself critically, if I watch my reactions, my concern for other persons, only during therapy sessions, and then in other places let myself go, simply because I can get away with it, then what? What am I getting away with? When I indulge myself, allow myself to be anything less or other than the person I am committed to being, I am simply being false to myself.

Should pastors escape to times and places where they can indulge themselves and not act like a pastor? That could be self-betrayal. What I discovered through search and effort is a new freedom—the freedom not to pretend, not to have to pretend. It's a real burden to pretend that I am what I am not. Deep down I know I will be discovered. Anxiety about such disclosure is hard to bear.

As the pastor of the church, the shepherd in the system, you must give up the pretenses of being what you are not, but in so doing you will discover the freedom to be what you are. Being yourself, you no longer need fear exposure as you live and interact in the system of the church. You can be yourself and still be a shepherd. Indeed, shepherding the system demands that you both be yourself and share who you are.

I know I am not consistent. Nor do I fail to reveal my faults and failures. Working with a system is in itself an exercise in self-revelation. I find forgiveness for my faults, but no tolerance for my pretense. As Mark Twain said, "your actions speak so loudly I cannot hear what you say." The system weds being with doing, and makes the marriage public. It helps impart to all of us, pastor and people alike, the "courage to be."

As shepherds of systems, therefore, you are called to be *more*. You are responsible to *be* more of yourself, more open, more free! Leaders lead by daring to model.

On the other hand, the shepherd of systems is *less!* The pastor has less power, less control, less responsibility, less authority. The leader avoids center stage; it is the system that reaps the glory and praise. The pastor receives less direct narcissistic gratification. The rewards are received through others. You do not know all and direct all. Your role is more modest—you are only part of the whole.

The Shepherd's Personal System

Pastors often complain of isolation. I believe that the complaint is frequently true, but the situation it bespeaks is unnecessary and undesirable. Pastors may exist in isolation from the church system because they have isolated themselves from it. It is unfortunate and sad when we cut ourselves off from a major system of nourishment and support. The systems model of ministry aims to restore the pastor to the parish, not only to serve the people, but to be served by them with a reciprocity that enables mutual growth.

The pastor also needs his or her own intimate psychosocial system. Every person has one. Such a system requires construction and maintenance. It should include not only family and parishioners but also close friends and colleagues. The pastor needs to develop a personal system that provides personal support. It may be helpful to look at your own psychosocial system. Which people do you find there? What are your relationships with these people? What are the problems in these relationships? How might you improve them? Seize the opportunity now to build your own necessary support.

Finally, the pastor needs to gain the perspective of fellow pastors. Pastoral fellowship means being responsible to each other, giving responsible feedback, reflection, and evaluation. Each pastor must be responsible for himself or herself. But to do so, one must have corrective insight, liberally shared by people of like faith and experience. Robert Burns was writing *To a Louse* when he said:

> Ah wad some power the giftie gie us
> To see oursels as others see us!
> It wad frae monie a blunder free us,
> An' foolish notion.

He could have been writing to pastors, for we need this gift as much as anyone—-and the church system helps to provide it for its shepherds.

I believe in the pastor. Indeed, much of this book consists of lessons I have learned from other pastors who have shared their thoughts, feelings, and experiences with me. In sharing we learn together. Here there is no room for professional dogma, only participation and growth. Personally, I am excited over these prospects for the pastorate. I hope you share the excitement.

Notes

Page
4. * Rollo May, "Values, Myths, and Symbols," *American Journal of Psychiatry* 132, no. 7 (1975): 703.
5. * The following books offer general introduction to social systems theory: Frederick K. Berrien, *General and Social Systems* (New Brunswick, N.J.: Rutgers University Press, 1968); Charles W. Churchman, *The Systems Approach* (New York: Delacorte, 1968); Kenneth de Greene, *Systems Psychology* (New York: McGraw-Hill, 1970); Marvin D. Mesaronic, *Views on General Systems Theory* (New York: Braziller, 1968); John M. Yinger, *Toward a Field Theory of Behavior* (New York: McGraw-Hill, 1965).
7. * Abraham Maslow, *Eupsychian Management* (Homewood, Ill.: Richard Irwin and The Dorsey Press, 1965), pp. 17–33, 88–107.
9. * For collected readings on applied organizational theory see: Harold W. Demone, Jr. and Dwight Harshbarger, eds., *A Handbook of Human Services Organizations* (New York: Behavioral Publications, 1974); Yeheskel Hasenfeld and Richard A. English, eds., *Human Service Organizations* (Ann Arbor: University of Michigan Press, 1974).
11. * Allen Wheelis, *The End of the Modern Age* (New York: Basic Books, 1971), p. 71.
12. * Prior descriptions of pastoral care from a systems view are given in: E. Mansell Pattison, "Systems Pastoral Care," *Journal of Pastoral Care* 26, no. 1 (1972): 2–14; Patrick T. Walsh, "Role of Chaplain as a Catalyst: In a System Theory Approach to the Delivery of Community Mental Health Services," *Association of Mental Health Chaplains Forum* 26, no. 1 (1973): 42–48.
15. * For description of early pioneers, development, and applications of group methodology see: E. Mansell Pattison, "Group Treatment Methods Suitable for Family Practice," *International Public Health Review* 2, no. 3 (1973): 247–65; and "Group Psychotherapy and Group Methods in Community Mental Health," *International Journal of Group Psychotherapy* 20, no. 4 (1970): 516–39.
15. † E. Mansell Pattison, "Psychosocial Predictors of Death Prognosis," *Omega* 5, no. 2 (1974): 145–60.
15. ‡ David Mendell, Stephen E. Cleveland, and Seymour Fisher, "A Five-Generation Family Theme," *Family Process* 7, no. 1 (1968): 127.
17. * Talcott Parsons, "The Kinship System of the Contemporary U.S.," *American Anthropologist* 45, no. 1 (1943): 22–38.
18. * Marvin B. Sussman, "The Isolated Nuclear Family: Fact or Fiction," *Social Problems* 6, no. 3 (1959): 334.
18. † The analysis and function of non-kin relationships is described in: Jeremy Boissevain, *Friends of Friends: Networks, Manipulators and Coalitions* (New York: St. Martin's Press, 1974); Hans Toch, *The Social Psychology of Social Movements* (Indianapolis: Bobbs-Merrill, 1964).
18. ‡ For extended theoretical research, and clinical discussion of social systems applications see: E. Mansell Pattison, "The Role of Adjunctive Therapies in Community Health Center Programs," *Therapeutic Recreation Journal* 3, no. 1 (1969): 16–25; "Social System Psychotherapy," *American Journal of Psychotherapy* 18, no. 4 (1973): 396–409; "Psychosocial System Therapy" in Ralph G. Hirschowitz and Bernard Levy, *The Changing Mental Health Scene* (New York: Spectrum Books, 1976), pp. 127–52.
31. * Richard H. Cox, ed., *Religious Systems and Psychotherapy* (Springfield, Ill.: C. C. Thomas, 1974).
35. * May, "Values, Myths, and Symbols."
37. * Clyde Kluckhohn, "Introduction," in William A. Less and Ezra Z. Vogt, eds., *Reader in Comparative Religion: An Anthropological Approach* (New York: Harper & Row, 1966), p. iii.

39. * Lawrence Kohlberg, "Development of Moral Character and Moral Ideology," in Martin S. and Lois W. Hoffman, eds., *Review of Child Development Research* (New York: Russell Sage Foundation, 1964),1: 284–310.

40. * Milton Rokeach, "Religious Values and Social Compassion," *Review of Religious Research* 11, no. 1 (1969): 39.

41. * For more detailed analysis of the psychological processes of morality see: Eric Fromm, *Escape from Freedom* (New York: Holt, Rinehart, & Winston, 1963), pp. 74ff.; E. Mansell Pattison, "Ego Morality: An Emerging Psychotherapeutic Concept," *Psychoanalytic Review* 55, no. 2 (1968): 186–222; "The Development of Moral Values in Children," *Pastoral Psychology* 20, no. 4 (1969): 14–30.

42. * Neil Postman and Charles Weingartner, *Teaching as a Subversive Activity* (New York: Delacorte Press, 1969), pp. 4–7.

45. * Howard J. Parad, ed., *Crisis Intervention: Selected Readings* (New York: Family Service Association of America, 1965).

49. * For further discussion of the shared roles of priest and physician see: E. Mansell Pattison, "Functions of the Clergy in Community Mental Health Centers," *Pastoral Psychology* 16, no. 5 (1965): 21–26; "Social and Psychological Aspects of Religion in Psychotherapy," *Journal of Nervous and Mental Diseases* 141, no. 2 (1966): 143–52; "The Chaplain in Community Mental Health: Agent of Program and Community," *Association of Mental Hospital Chaplains Newsletter* 23, no. 3 (1970): 14–25.

52. * For extended analysis of healing transactions see: Arthur K. Shapiro, "A Contribution to a History of the Placebo Effect," *Behavioral Science* 5, no. 1 (1960): 109–35; E. Mansell Pattison, Nickolajs A. Lapins, and Hans O. Doerr, "Faith Healing: A Study of Personality and Function," *Journal of Nervous and Mental Diseases* 157, no. 3 (1973): 397–409.

53. * Francis W. Peabody, "The Care of the Patient," *Journal of the American Medical Association* 88, no. 8 (1927): 882.

53. † Erik Erikson, "The Golden Rule and the Cycle of Life," *Harvard Medical Alumni Bulletin* (Winter 1963), p. 9.

54. * Sigmund Freud, *The Future of an Illusion*, vol. 21, *Collected Works* (London: Hogarth Press, 1961).

64. * Robert C. Leslie, "Helping the Theological Student to Dare to Be Himself," in Hans Hoffman, *The Ministry and Mental Health* (New York: Association Press, 1960), pp. 127–42.

67. * Edgar W. Mills, "Intentionality and the Ministry," *Journal of Pastoral Care* 28, no. 2 (1974): 82.

71. * Douglas W. Orr, "Transference and Countertransference: A History Survey," *Journal of the American Psychoanalytic Association* 2, no. 4 (1954): 261–70.

72. * Karl Menninger, *Theory of Psychoanalytic Technique* (New York: Basic Books, 1958), p. 10.

74. * Ernest M. Rosenzweig, "The Minister and Congregation: A Study in Ambivalence," *Psychoanalytic Review* 2, no. 2 (1941): 218–28.

74. † Jean Piaget, *The Moral Judgment of the Child* (New York: Harcourt, 1932).

79. * For interesting and insightful descriptions of the psychodynamic uses of the pastoral role see: Earl A. Grollman, "Some Sights and Insights of History, Psychology, and Psychoanalysis Concerning the Father-God and Mother-Goddess Concepts of Judaism and Christianity," *American Image* 20, no. 2 (1962): 187–212; Charles G. Schoenfeld, "God the Father—and Mother: Study and Extension of Freud's Conception of God as an Exalted Father," ibid., pp. 213–34; Ernest Jones, "The God Complex," in *Essays in Applied Psychoanalysis* (London: Hogarth Press, 1951): 2: 54–71.

80. * Elaine Cumming and Charles Harrington, "Clergyman as Counselor," *American Journal of Sociology* 63, no. 2 (1963): 234–44.

80. † Richard V. McCann, *The Churches and Mental Health* (New York: Basic Books, 1962).

Annotated Bibliography

Dittes, James E. *The Church in th(*
1967. An investigation of *th*
ish, with specific attention to th(/
parishioners and church organizatio./
Kilinski, Kenneth, and Wofford, Jerry. (./
Christian Church. Grand Rapids: Zonderv./
proach to systematic planning and definition (.
personal examples of organizational structure and (./
Leas, Speed, and Kittlaus, Paul. *Church Fights: Manag(. /*
Local Church. Philadelphia: Westminster, 1973. A manua. /
and laity offering strategies not for avoidance but for resolution /
which is seen as creative and growth producing.
Mead, Lauren B. *New Hope for Congregations.* New York: Seabury, 1. /
Case studies from the Episcopal project "Test Pattern," in which congregations seeking a new pastor are assisted in setting goals and priorities, and in
defining the purposes of their church ministry.
Pattison, E. Mansell, ed. *Clinical Psychiatry and Religion.* Boston: Little,
Brown & Co., 1969. Practical essays on the relationship between mental
health and the church, with sections on the interpretation of religion, religious behavior, mental health of clergy, and collaboration between clergy
and mental health professionals.
Schaller, Lyle. *The Change Agent.* New York: Seabury, 1972. One of many
books by this author addressed to the parish ministry, with focus on the
problems of church change, resistance to change, and the role and functions of the pastor as a change agent.
Seifert, Harvey, and Clinebell, Howard J., Jr. *Personal Growth and Social
Change.* Philadelphia: Westminster, 1969. Examines the potential for personal growth in the church through both intimate group experiences and
the social tasks and actions of the church.
Smith, Donald P. *Caught in the Crossfire.* Philadelphia: Westminster, 1973.
Describes tensions in the church—between priorities, commitments, and
the various constituencies—that place the pastor in the center of church
conflict, with examples of creative leadership in the midst of cross-purposes.